With *The Authenticity Experiment: Lessons From The Best &
Worst Year Of My Life*, Kate Carroll de Gutes has written a
masterful navigation of the human soul in both crisis and
wonder. This collection of essays, written as an exercise of
introspection and transparency in an era of cosmetic
sincerity, combine to illuminate the complex landscape of a
true artist's mind through tragedy and fleeting completion.
De Gutes' pilgrimage in the process of grief attempts to
either make desperate sense of the chaos in the vacuum of
loss, or cling to those transient moments when things are,
unexpectedly, crystallized — albeit briefly — in perfection,
or the memory of perfection. Kate's care for both language
and craft, along with her gifts for insight, profound
observation and wit, will resonate in the heart and mind of
the reader for days afterward. It's an incredible work worthy
of sharing a book shelf with Joan Didion. Kate's voice and
heart will resonate among the best memoirists of our age.

— Domingo Martinez, author of *The Boy Kings of Texas*

ॐ

Kate Carroll de Gutes decided to spend a while doing what
most of us don't do: tell the truth. Tell the truth to herself
and then to everyone else, and the truth turns out to be
funny, hard, sad, sweet, tough, confusing, tender and sharp.
It's your truth, too.

—Sallie Tisdale, author of eight books, including
Violation, Talk Dirty to Me, and *Stepping Westward*

॥

Kate Carroll de Gutes is the Annie Leibovitz of short essays. Most blog posts last as long as Snapchats, but *The Authenticity Experiment: Lessons From The Best & Worst Year Of My Life*—like stylized portraits—renders what can't be seen, only felt. They offer readers a way to see, really see, and to love. With images like a scowling baby hawk and the ever-present Cannondale bike, she works through grief and marvels at its grit. What she captures in these works of art testifies to memories and friendships that endure longer than the living.

  — Kate Gray, author of *Carry The Sky*

॥

Kate Carroll de Gutes' extraordinary *The Authenticity Experiment* demands an authentic quote. Reading it, which I did very slowly so as to savor each tiny, beautiful chapter, I thought: "Oh, oh, oh, this is so good. Oh! I love this! This woman can WRITE. How on earth has she composed a book about dying and grieving that radiates with so much joy, life, and humor? Okay, I'm buying a copy for everyone I know." You should too.

  — Karen Karbo, author of *The Gospel According to Coco Chanel*

THE AUTHENTICITY EXPERIMENT

Lessons from
the Best and Worst Year of My Life

Sarah —

Thank you,

thank you,

thank you.

#DarkAndLight

THE AUTHENTICITY EXPERIMENT

Lessons from
the Best and Worst Year of My Life

KATE CARROLL DE GUTES

Two Sylvias Press

Two Sylvias Press
PO Box 1524
Kingston, WA 98346
twosylviaspress@gmail.com

Cover Design: Kelli Russell Agodon
Book Design: Annette Spaulding-Convy
Author Photo Credit: Jules Hays Norton

Two Sylvias Press would like to thank the following publishers and individuals for granting permission to use their work:
Carrie Newcomer and Available Light Publishing
Gregory Orr and Copper Canyon Press
Deb Talan and ASCAP

Created with the belief that *great writing is good for the world*, Two Sylvias Press mixes modern technology, classic style, and literary intellect with an eco-friendly heart. We draw our inspiration from the poetic literary talent of Sylvia Plath and the editorial business sense of Sylvia Beach. We are an independent press dedicated to publishing the exceptional voices of writers.

For more information about Two Sylvias Press or to learn more about the eBook version of *The Authenticity Experiment* please visit:
www.twosylviaspress.com

First Edition. Created in the United States of America.

ISBN: 13: 978-0998631417

Two Sylvias Press
www.twosylviaspress.com

To Barbara
and to Erin
for illuminating a path through the dark.

And, of course, to Sue and Jule for walking the path
with me.

Table of Contents

III. Winter

IV. Spring

V. Summer

Foreword

Kate Carroll de Gutes is working in one of the slipperiest contemporary forms—the blog—a form that so closely narrates the stuff of one's days it can easily slip into diary mode, feel merely occasional, or indulge in cringy acts of "sharing." Though Facebook is particularly constructed to deliver shiny, handpicked moments, to use any of our contemporary platforms meaningfully requires enormous deftness. In *The Authenticity Experiment*, you'll find not a whiff of the posed or the stretched, no gatherings of flawless friends, or snapshots of Mensa-worthy pets, or to-die-for new clothes modeled on sunny verandas (though you will encounter a gorgeous ode to a spectacular and complex tux.) *The Authenticity Experiment* is an act of recovery, a thorough reimagining of the medium, a way of imprinting surface with depth, lighting up daily moments by slowing and shaping them into truly beautiful meditations.

What Kate does in these posts/essays/entries from the very beginning is privilege moments. She interrogates the very instance of sitting to write, searches out the look and feel, and commits to getting the flash of it down. What might that moment of sitting to write contain? A hospital room in which a beloved is taking her long leave. Love letters. Portraits of intimates and strangers. Rages. Instructions. Eulogies. And more. Looking hard of course can take many forms, depending on one's sensibility and the way one is inclined to turn the light on a certain subject. Though the collection focuses on grief and loss, these pieces are anything but darkened or insular. Here, to be stricken by grief, is also to notice the angle of light striking a face, an hour, a hard-won moment of peace-within-chaos. Kate's sensibility recognizes grief's shifting and complex registers, and the way it shades into wonder, compassion (both the giving and accepting of), gratitude (in huge measures), forgiveness, awe, and more. The long aftermath of profound loss, encounters with "improbable grace" (with, say, strangers in "mustard colored, double front Carhartts"), the recalled scent of herbs in a room that hauls a past era into the present—these are made to matter because Kate honors, above all, her writerly intentions. She holds to a core, self-defined project—the "experiment"—so that each treasured instance, image, or idea is treated with curiosity, and no outcome is fixed or certain. The result of her approach is a keen sense of surprise—discoveries that are fresh for both writer and reader.

Over and over again, Kate posits challenges to herself (one rousing beginning goes: "I spent the afternoon going through dead peoples' things") and then… she dives. Flails around. Lets herself splash. Finds a steady stroke. Finds her balance. Pulls you close in and then … tells it like it is. Her ease is the kind that exists between friends and intimates, wherein one trusts that the other wants to hear what's being said. Of course, that desire to listen is cultivated in a friend or in a reader by being an adept listener oneself. Kate's a gifted listener, tuned in to the geographies of others' griefs and joys as well. This is a gorgeous, openhearted book, a pilgrim's map to those hidden spots where authentic experiences await anyone brave enough to look for them.

– Lia Purpura

Prologue

I started writing *The Authenticity Experiment* as a blog when my friend the poet Fleda Brown returned to Facebook after a hiatus and asked her community how they felt when they saw nothing but curated posts full of pictures of risotto, fantastic family vacations, and lots of "Hail, fellow, well met!" status updates. And, I thought, yeah, we don't like to talk about our dark on social media, do we. In fact, you could argue that we don't like to talk about our dark at all. I certainly was guilty of what Fleda asked about: touting my first book, sharing pictures of my bike rides, maybe even a couple of pictures of zucchini noodle pasta (no risotto for me, too carb heavy). Fleda made me wonder if I could tell the truth—the whole truth—on social media for thirty days.

My mentor and editor, Judith Kitchen, said she thought that social media had become the new back fence, the place where we stand and talk to our "neighbors" and tell them the good and the bad, the truth about our days and our lives. I think she's right, but the problem is we don't really share our whole selves at this digital back fence. Yet if we're going to continue to hang out here and share our lives digitally, we do need to share more, much more. Not everything, but at least a well-balanced bit of #DarkAndLight. You're wondering about that hashtag? That's how I ended all of my posts, which were actually short essays. Because I hoped they showed the duality—the both/and, the dark/light—of life.

I wrote every day no matter what. Sometimes I didn't post until 11:30 p.m., but with the exception of one very bad day, I wrote. In the middle of this experiment, my mother—who had Alzheimer's and was across town from me in assisted living—began having strokes and actively dying. Because the facility did not want a death on their books, the manager insisted we move my mother. So ten days before she died, my sisters and I moved my mother to an adult foster home. And still I wrote.

When the thirty days were up, people wondered if I would continue. Something about my voice and my experience tapped into the cultural current. Most of my Facebook friends are between the ages of thirty-five and sixty. We're all facing changing bodies, dying parents, midlife divorces, and career changes. I just put voice to these common experiences. Cathy Brown, who has been my friend since eighth grade, wrote, "What I love most about these posts is your wonderful ability to shine a light on such meaningful moments, bringing them to the forefront of the everyday life we lead. I have many of these moments, (memories, thoughts and emotions) and nothing to do with them."

I continued writing after the thirty days were up but dropped back to one or two longer essays per week. *The Authenticity Experiment* became a place to share and express my grief. To show the world what closing two estates looked like—yes, two, because six months before my mother died, my best friend died and I served as executor for her estate as well—and also to share the good and the bittersweet—because my first book, *Objects In Mirror Are Closer Than They Appear,* edited by Judith Kitchen, won the Oregon Book Award for Creative Nonfiction and the Lambda Literary Award for Memoir. But Judith didn't live to see this. Nor did my mother, my father, or my best friend. Yet this experience, these awards were huge and fantastic and amazing and unexpected.

And there it is right there—the duality of my life, of

all our lives. The best and worst year of my life all rolled together. Because that's what life is. In real life and on the page, I wanted to, as the writer Courtney E. Martin says, "[Show] up whole despite all the risks." She goes on to say, "It takes a certain kind of modern courage to stop crafting. To say, enough with the curation. Enough with the control. I'm just going to be myself."

The essays you'll find in this book are raw and filtered through my lens as I think on the page and try to understand the journey I'm on and how my own privilege and power plays a role in what I think about death, class, self-worth, perfectionism, and other topics we usually keep to ourselves. I don't offer any answers, and I don't always find my way to conclusions, or to better thinking. It's like hacking a path through the forest: you can't always see where you're going, and you can't always see how far you've come, but you know you're on your way to somewhere.

– Kate Carroll de Gutes

I.

Summer

THE DARK AND THE LIGHT

My friend who appears rough and tumble tough but is really just the most tender and gentle soul wrapped in six feet said to me, "Is it okay to be mad?" She was talking about all the clowns in the world and cancer and death and the unfairness of the dark mornings in the northern latitudes, particularly on days when the espresso machine is acting finicky, and how we have to keep moving forward even as we are surrounded by idiots (some of them well-meaning) who say crap like, "At least she is peaceful," or "He's in a better place now," or, godfuckingdforbid, "Now your parents are together again." As if they knew our parents. As if our parents would want that.

And I responded that of course, of course it is okay to be mad! That we should feel mad about so much injustice and grief and pain. That we must stop outsourcing our dark and own it. Because that's what we as a culture do, outsource all our negative feelings.

Go ahead and name them: anger, anxiety, despair, envy, grief, guilt, hate, regret, shame. The list is longer, but those are the biggies that we run from, aren't they? And where do we put these emotions? On television, in the movies, in our politics, on Facebook and Twitter. Instead of owning our anxiety and fear, we watch *Law and Order: SVU*.

Instead of dealing with our own frustration at the seemingly never-ending tasks of modern living (*Why is my calendar buzzing with an appointment right now? What is that email about?*), we watch movies like *True Grit* or anything by Quentin Tarantino. Instead of pulling apart the duality of our current political system, we post on Facebook that Donald Trump is an asshat rather than trying to understand why the message of said asshat resonates with so many people.

And then, just to make things worse, we glorify the ridiculous obverse of all this dark. We slip on the ice and break our tailbones and, instead of crying and feeling frustrated by the injury and the never-melting sheet of ice on the front steps, we say, "Well, I suppose this forces me to slow down." But, as Debbie Ford says in her book, *The Dark Side of the Light Chasers*, "Even if you choose to hide your dark side, it will still cast a shadow. Only by owning every aspect of yourself can you achieve harmony. . . . The purpose of doing shadow work is to become whole. To end our suffering."

The well-known and revered Jungian analyst Marion Woodman says, "Our shadow may contain the best parts of ourselves." But we're projecting this shadow outside. We're not owning it, not healing this supposed rift in ourselves. We're failing to make ourselves whole.

But the dark is infinitely human and natural. Just ask Persephone, who spent six months in the dark underworld with Hades. So be mad. Be profoundly sad. Be angry. Be envious. Be all of this! You won't be graded on smiling through your pain or swallowing your anger until your guts are a wreck or you are drinking away your anxiety. You will only be graded on how honest you were. Because, in the end, authenticity matters most.

HELLO, MY NAME IS …

I have nicknames for many of my beloveds. Not all of them, for sure. The name has to arise organically and in its own time. But in this book—as in the online versions of these essays—the people I write about, by and large, are identified by nicknames because they didn't necessarily sign up to have their lives spread across the page and the Internet simply because we are friends and they love me. The people you meet in these pages include the Alaskan Poet, the Blonde Bombshell, the Child Barista, the Country Music Singing Femme, the Designer Gay, the Dudes, the Idaho Playwright, the Ironman, Lesbiana Profundis, my Lesbro, the Opera Singer, the Sailor, my Secret Weapon, the Tines, the Very Important Poet, and the Woman Who Is Not My Girlfriend. These names, I think, capture the essence of my friends, family, and colleagues—my beloveds—and I use them, as I said, because it is hard to love a nonfiction writer, but also because I think they paint a picture of who each person is at their core. Do these people recognize themselves? Sure. Would you recognize them on the street? Maybe.

ৰু

My ex-wife did not get her nickname until we had been together six years. Then a piece of mail arrived— remember real, honest-to-goodness mail?—that was addressed to Judy Simonsap. This slayed me, so I can still remember the way I laughed. I started calling her Sap shortly after that because the mail amused me so much and also because it fit her personality. She cried at Hallmark commercials and wept at that Folger's Coffee commercial where the daughter arrives home early for Christmas and makes coffee for her whole family, but only her dad wakes up and they share a moment. And all she had to do was hear the music for that McDonald's commercial where the little old man went back to work flipping burgers because he missed connecting with people, and she'd begin tearing up. (In her defense, that damn McDonald's commercial got me every time, too.)

There is also my friend Biz. Biz is short for Busy Gal, which Biz is and always has been. Biz has been Biz so long that another friend of mine recently turned to her at one of my readings and said, "I forget your real name."

I have a client called Jesus because he is a fundamentalist Christian who once slammed his palm on the table and shouted, "I'm the client, and I'm always right!" And I also work with a narcissistic and evil business colleague I call the Devil because she would step across your bleeding and mangled body if it got her more work.

Back in the nineties I once sent my ex-wife a text message—in the early days when you had to tap 84433 just to spell *the*—that said, "The Chinese Grandma was cooking in her garage and it caught on fire. Diane put it out with the Serial Killer's hose. I called 911. Very exciting." While culturally insensitive, my ex-wife could picture exactly what happened. Admittedly, I could have probably called the grandma by her name (if I had known it) or picked up the phone and called too.

But the Chinese Grandma really was that—a grandma who was Chinese and spoke virtually no English— and after twenty years of living at that house, we still never knew her name, so we called her the Chinese Grandma. She always fried food in a wok in her garage so the house didn't smell like grease. This day, though, she had the wok balanced

4

precariously on her yellow recycle bin. While she hunched down on her heels, the wok shifted and the hot oil ignited the paper in the bin, the grandma's hair, and the garage door frame. Her house and the Serial Killer's shared a common driveway and their garages were connected. It was logical to use his hose.

Oh, you're wondering about the Serial Killer's name? He never talked to any of us. Not once in the ten years he lived there. And he never opened his drapes. He'd do his yard work very early in the morning or late at night, and if it looked like any of us were coming over to talk to him, he'd drop his implements and run inside. At least that is how I remember it. And you know how when it is discovered that someone is a serial killer and the news reporters interview the neighbors, they always say, "He was such a quiet man."

But that neighborhood was good. Sarah and Sheldon and then Fred and Sandy lived next door. Joe lived on the other corner, and Nosy Netta and her henpecked husband Mr. Netta (seriously, I don't even know Mr. Netta's real name) lived across from Joe. Everyone watched out for the Chinese Grandma and Grandpa, and if their grown kids weren't around to translate for the UPS guy or the fire department, we'd try and help. At night people sat on their porches and porch swings, and friends and neighbors dropped by for a visit.

We weren't pervasively connected by text or Facebook then. We actually had to call or drop by to get the news. In fact, in the days of the Serial Killer, we still had an answering machine because we liked to screen our calls. Do you even know what that means? Have you ever heard a disembodied voice shouting, "Pick up! It's important! Pick up!"

I miss those times, and I don't think it's because I am nostalgic. I miss hanging out and just chatting, setting an extra plate for whoever happens to show up around dinnertime (Carol and Kate, I'm thinking of you). Things did not feel so frantic then. If I had to give our time now a nickname, it would be Frenenzia, a fusion of *frantic*, *frenetic*, and *mania*. I don't think it's healthy. I'm guilty of it even as I want it to change—checking email when I excuse myself from the table to go to the restroom, sending a quick text while I wait at a traffic light, swiping left and sending you to voicemail when I really should just pick up. But it's important, the connection. And I think it's time I shut off the phone and the data plan and picked up where we left off.

WISH YOU WERE HERE

I drove to Bend, Oregon, for a book reading in the town I rarely visit anymore. While I love it here, it feels painful, partly because of the life I lost here and partly because . . . well, I don't know exactly. I think that I always wanted to live some place like Bend or Jackson or Sun Valley, where nature is right outside your door, ready to heal and instruct.

And I think, until about ten minutes ago, that I had a huge projection going on the people who live in Bend, or in towns like this. That they are healthy, happy, balanced athletes. Maybe they are. But as I heard from people at my reading, just as many of them are struggling to find love and pay bills in a town where the median home price is $320,000 and rising 8.5 percent per quarter, a town where to have $1 million you need to start with $2 million (cue the cymbals).

I guess I think it's painful because I would have tried to fit myself into this life I thought I wanted, but would have been stuck because I would have always been dissatisfied. Because almost everyone would have more money, a nicer house in a better location, a better body with a better tan, be a better athlete, et cetera, et cetera, et cetera. I would have been caught in my own comparison loop and would never be happy with the life I had.

On my drive over, I heard this quote from Seth Godin. I think it speaks to where I find myself: "Giving the people what they want isn't nearly as powerful as teaching people what they need. . . . When we change our culture in this direction, we're doing work that's worth sharing. But it's slow going. If it were easy, it would have happened already."

So yeah, I could have probably found someone to buy me a big $750,000 house on the Deschutes, and I could wake up every morning and smell the vanilla scent of the ponderosas and listen to the mourning doves sing their plaintive song, but then I'd probably still find myself in this spot at some point, asking what it was that I really wanted. What is the projection I'm holding on this place, these people, this life? And how much harder would the inevitable crash be if I were enmeshed in this life?

So instead I'll have dinner on the river with a dear, authentic friend who will laugh kindly and with recognition when I tell her all this. I'll enjoy the river, the view, the town for what they are: beautiful and a nice place to visit.

MISLED

Facebook misleads us, doesn't it? With our curated lives, partial images of what's going on. My own feed shows me at the Pink Martini concert dancing to China Forbes singing "Brazil." And riding my red Cannondale CAAD 10 on the Deschutes River Trail (note the fine components on my bike and my amazing cycling kit). And at Spork eating an appropriately sized, gluten-free, cruelty-free, low-carb lunch with five of my close friends.

That's why I started this experiment. Could I show you the full picture? Could I bare my soul that way? Tell you that the bike shorts are a size larger than last year. Disclose that the concert made me nostalgic for a night eighteen years ago when my ex-wife and I first bought *Sympathique* and blasted it through our Optimus bookshelf speakers and out into our backyard with the newly-finished cobblestone patio replete with black wrought iron furniture. That I remember that night and the gin and tonic with such longing for what was so good about that time and place and relationship.

Things were easier, or so I thought. People dropped by and parties happened spontaneously—great big Barefoot Contessa–type meals on that patio. And my ex-wife and I talked well into the night about things that felt so important—feel so important—books, news, the future, the garden.

On the Deschutes River bike ride, though, my friend Lesbiana Profundis and I talked about our former marriages and how what we think we really miss is the *idea* of what we thought our marriages were. In other words, we miss the story that we told ourselves about our relationships. Because the reality is, I drank way too much during that entire marriage. The reasons why are myriad, but the fact remains, during those Barefoot Contessa meals, I had a big buzz on. But in the picture of my marriage I remembered during the Pink Martini concert, that's conveniently Photoshopped out.

Everything is both/and. You either embrace it or you hate it. Sometimes you do both. We live in the great mess, the *humus*, or soil, of life—which has for its root, the same prefix as human. It comes from the Latin *homo* (not *that homo*, that's Greek), which means to be born of the earth. Life should be dirty, tumbling around in all the organic components that make up our lives, our living, ashes to ashes, and all that beautiful fertileness that makes us who we are. We should not Photoshop it out just so we look a little happier, a little skinnier, and like we had one less gin and tonic. Take a breath and embrace the duality, and remember, it's okay if your bike shorts are a size larger than last year.

SITTING ALONE

I have a lot of very good friends. I'm lucky that way. So many people struggle with deep loneliness and a feeling of not mattering to anyone. And it's not that I don't ever feel this way, but on more days than not, there is someone I can call or email, but usually call, to talk through the hard stuff: my mom, my job, my art, my finances (or lack thereof), my love life (or lack thereof), my motivation for the gym (or lack thereof). You get the point. My phone and email trees are full of branches laden with support.

But there was a 2011 study done by Cornell University that showed in the years since 1985, the average number of close friendships has declined from three to only two—despite people's Facebook networks having hundreds of friends. The sociologist, Matthew Brashears, interviewed two thousand people and asked them to list the names of people with whom they had discussed "important matters" in the last six months, and 48 percent of the respondents listed just one name, 18 percent listed two names, and only 29 percent listed more than two. A sad 4 percent listed no one.

My friend Stef fell into the 48 percent. But by some accounts, she also fell into the 4 percent. I met Stef in July of 1994. We worked together at my only corporate job. She was eighteen years older, but we both had Midwestern roots, a similar sense of humor, and, in the ways of good friends, the same tender spots that showed up in the exact opposite way in each other, so we innately understood each other. In some ways, Stef saw me much more clearly than I ever saw her. I remember one time when work pressure threatened to kill us both. Stef turned to me and said, "Go to a movie right now." I allowed as how I couldn't go to a movie in the middle of the workday. She reminded me I had a pager and could always "burn a quarter" returning a page and no one but she would know where I was calling from. (Remember those days? Remember paging someone with 911 on the end so they'd know to respond immediately? And responding from a payphone—hence "burning a quarter." So much technological change in such a short time.) So I did. I went to a movie. I still remember what I watched: *The Mask* with Jim Carrey. I returned, if not refreshed, at least more sane, just like Stef knew I would.

But just as I wasn't suited to corporate life, neither was she. Full of anxiety, full of fears of perfectionism, and unable to prioritize information (looking back, I wonder if Stef had ADD), shortly after I left, the management pushed Stef out, and she fell so completely apart that she didn't really leave the house for two full years except for doctor's appointments and therapy.

Then, in 2007, Stef's husband, Ron, dropped dead of a heart attack. Stef, traveling for a new job she hated, was gone the night he died. She had called Ron that evening, and when he didn't answer, she got a bad feeling and lay in her cheap hotel room—maybe the La Quinta Inn or perhaps the Ramada, at any rate, something near Sea-Tac airport—and she cried and cried and cried. But she didn't call her neighbors, Cheryl or Shari, and she didn't call me—whom she called her best friend—to go check on Ron. The story, as you might imagine from episodes of *NYPD Blue*, ended predictably.

Shortly after, Stef quit her job. The reasons are both imaginable and unimaginable. Because, in addition to losing Ron, two of Stef's cats also died that year, her water line broke and flooded her yard and left her liable for a $4,000 water bill, and her car started acting up. When a bully at work started hammering on Stef, pulling her out of the company's holiday party to give her a Personal Improvement Plan, Stef snapped and quit. I couldn't really blame her. By and large, she managed all this by herself.

She didn't really have the money not to work, but she wasn't quite able to work either. She'd inherited about $200,000 in life insurance from Ron, but that was all there was. On the day he died, at age sixty, Ron had saved a sum total of $23,000 for retirement. As I said, not working wasn't really an option for her.

I took Stef to two different financial planners so she could invest her money. This was in early 2008, and the market had not yet crashed. Stef didn't really trust the financial planners, and she didn't exactly trust me either. Or she did, but she was such a mess, she couldn't make up her mind. One of the financial planners—the one I didn't like and she did—put the fear of god into her and told her to put everything in annuities making like 3.75 percent a year. I tried to explain to her why this was a bad idea, but she just couldn't think clearly. So she did nothing.

Until one day in 2012. After burning through most of the money, she called the annuities planner and dumped the last of it in an annuity. She'd been drawing down her dead husband's IRA every month and paying taxes, penalties, and an agency fee for each withdrawal. She never asked me if this was a good idea and Thrivent Financial for Lutherans—the asshats—never offered her anything else.

Stef and I had dinner once a month and talked on the phone once a week. I'd check in on her; she'd check in on me (well, mostly, it was the former). But when the Opera Singer left me for a married man (bonus: two ruined marriages for the price of one!), Stef became a lifeline. I'd call her and sometimes just show up at her house crying and so fucked up. I remember sitting in her family room, in these little yellow swivel chairs she'd bought after she remodeled the house without asking anybody if they thought it was a good use of her money. (As an aside, I now totally understand the post-death remodel. I have a new master closet, hickory floors, blackout blinds, and new fir doors with frosted glass inserts. It's like you must do something to shift the energy in a house that feels as if it's trapped in the dark.)

The chairs in Stef's redesigned family room were set up facing each other, somewhat like a traditional therapist's office, and I used my right leg to push myself back and forth, the movement comforting me as I cried out my pain and my shame. In a way, this was mine and Stef's most powerful connection: our secret beliefs that we were unworthy of love for one reason or another. We never talked about this, but we saw how that sore spot looked in each other and danced carefully around it.

After Ron's death, Stef named me her healthcare representative, financial power of attorney, and executor should something happen. She was my emergency contact for all things medical, and I wore her name on a bracelet each time I cycled. She knew all my surgeries and allergies and that my mother had had a heart attack before age sixty. You know, all those things that doctors ask and someone must answer.

I took Stef to the hospital a couple of times for heart procedures. She'd had a mitral valve replacement, a pacemaker, and cardioversion for A-fib. But more times than not, Stef took herself and called me ex post facto. Each time I'd get mad and cry, and she'd say, "I'd call you if it was really big."

So when the phone rang on December 15 and it was

the Providence trunk line—which I recognized from the twenty years my ex-wife worked at the hospital—I knew it was Stef. I said, "This is Kate." She said, "Kate this is . . ." and I interrupted, "Are you in the ER or have you been admitted?" She hated that I knew and that I left the Christmas party I was supposed to attend to come to the hospital.

The story gets long and convoluted, but suffice it to say that Stef had been in pain for a couple of months. And it took another month of her in her quiet, unassuming way and then me in my big, brash, pay-the-fuck-attention-to-my-friend-or-I'll-sue-your-goddamned-asses way before we got a diagnosis of stage IV lung cancer.

Or rather, before Stef got a diagnosis, because she was alone when she got that diagnosis. At the time I sat on a Mexican beach on a much-needed vacation that she insisted I not cancel because I was so fried from caregiving for my mom. And when she went in for the thoracentesis and bronchoscopy, the procedures that gave her a definitive diagnosis, she went alone. She didn't want to bother the neighbors, and there was no one else to call.

The good news—if there is good news when it comes to cancer and the inevitable—is that Stef didn't die alone. I held her hand and prayed her out the whole way, telling her I loved her and that her cat and I would be just fine.

We are starting to feel better even though we've lost one person on our phone tree.

LETTING THE WORDS WASH OVER YOU

Just two months before my mom died, Ovenbird Books published my first book, *Objects In Mirror Are Closer Than They Appear*. The publisher and editor was my friend and mentor, Judith Kitchen, and she died just two days after finishing her edit of my manuscript. Judith asked and asked for that manuscript. But the story I told myself was that I'd written it to satisfy the requirements for my Master of Fine Arts, that it was fine as a thesis, not as a book.

Before my mom moved to Portland, before we knew how compromised her memory was, she read the thesis and said, "You know, honey, I don't look very nice in this." The way I remember it, she sounded pained and small. I recall the day as gray, the Levolors open, the heavy cloud cover of the Olympics pressing in on the house, but that could have just been my own fear pushing in on me in that moment. I think I said, *I'm sorry*. I didn't know what else to say. In hindsight, I know for certain this affected my desire for publication. I couldn't bear her chagrin at the picture I'd painted of her and her marriage—didn't want to hurt her that way in the larger world—so I censored myself and let the manuscript languish in an electronic drawer, if you will, until Judith finally convinced me otherwise.

By the time the book—substantially revised—was released, my mother had lost the ability to read, not entirely, but words didn't always make sense to her. Sometimes she'd read a letter again and again, and I'd ask her if she wanted me to read it to her because often the *story* read aloud to her made sense where the words did not. "No," she'd say, "I'm just letting the words wash over me and I'm feeling them."

No writer could argue with that.

Still, I felt grateful she couldn't read the book itself

because I knew that there were parts that would hurt her. One of her caregivers, Star, an amazing young woman we hired to just hang with my mom, read her select essays—Star knew which ones were off-limits. I think my mom liked this. On the night of my book launch in Portland, we planned for Star to bring my mom. Star arrived at my mother's apartment two and a half hours before they needed to leave for the reading. She was going to help my mom get dressed, apply her makeup, cue her over and over on the event. Then ten minutes before the reading was scheduled to begin, Star called and said they weren't coming; my mom had been combative all afternoon and still wasn't ready. My mom got on the phone and said she was sorry, but she was just so tired, she didn't think she could manage the reading. I also knew she felt terrified of the social situation, of forgetting names of people she should know, of feeling overwhelmed by the noise and was worried what the book said about her. She could not have known that I'd carefully chosen what to read, pieces that didn't touch on my family, pieces where she'd laugh and not grimace.

After I hung up the phone, I didn't cry, feeling instead a profound heaviness in my heart. But I'll tell you now, I'm crying as I type this. I wanted her there in the way that we always want our mothers to see us succeed. And I wanted her there because she was so proud of me and the book even as some part of her brain still feared what I'd written. A stack of my books sat on the end of her couch, so she could loan them out to caregivers. "This is my daughter's book," she'd say and push the book forward into an outstretched hand.

To me she'd say, "Oh, honey, I'm so glad I lived to see this." And even as I also felt scared of what was on the page, I was glad she was still alive too.

Now, one of the first questions people ask me is, "Does it feel great having a book out?"

The short answer is sort of. Like all things, it's both/and. My book is done, and I'm pleased with it, and I think it's pretty good. And I'm also aware that I'm standing completely naked—as it were—in public, and people are reading the work and judging both the content and the craft.

It's my friends and family I most want to like it. But I know better than to ask what they think about it. Because, what if they hate it? Or don't remember the stories the same way? Or what if my grad school friends think it's poorly written?

I don't really care much what random strangers think—or, rather, I don't really care *that* much. When I read in Bend, I was pleased that people seemed to resonate with my work, but I only sold four copies of the book, which wasn't even enough to pay for the gas over the mountain. Did I choose the wrong pieces? Should I have read the piece about driving and hiking and kayaking in Baja to the sporty Bend crowd? Or should I simply relish that I sold four books? Maybe I should stop looking at my sales and rankings altogether.

Last week I listened to Maria Popova in conversation with Krista Tippett. Tippett does a show I've listened to for years called *On Being*. It's on the NPR feed or you can listen via podcast, which is what I usually do. Anyways, Popova said, "We live in an era where . . . you can see things like Facebook likes and retweets . . . I mean, they are right there. And I think it takes a real discipline just to not hang the stability of your soul on them."

So, I'm trying not to be crazy about tracking sales or

reviews. My family and friends like my book very much in most cases. That's what really matters to me. But I admit that I find myself wanting to have 173 thumbs-up on the picture of me reading in Portland or in Bend or garner 47 comments on each *Authenticity Experiment* essay I've posted. I'm driven by competition. I think it's innate to my personality. I'm always trying to best myself. But I don't think it's healthy. It's a kind of addiction to perfection. And nothing is truly perfect. It never can be.

What happened to good enough? What happened to sharing a story over the digital fence and not striving for likes? Or putting a book out there into the world and not slaving for a *New York Times* review? When did being average stop being okay? I'm not saying one shouldn't have goals, but let's remember our old pal Wordsworth, "Getting and spending we lay waste our powers," and maybe take a breath and a break.

TUMBLING INTO THE EVER-PRESENT NOW

Someone recently suggested I start writing a few essays about Alzheimer's. It could be because I said my next book is going to be about Alzheimer's. It could also be that I said I was afraid to write about this—my experience with my mom and my own fears that I might be losing my mind. It could be because I'm always imploring people to write about what scares them, and turnabout is fair play. It's hard to say.

Maybe one of the reasons I haven't written about this is that I try to make meaning out of everything, which is—*duh*—what writers do, but in this case, I can't. I simply cannot make meaning out of Alzheimer's. Can't understand why the Alaskan Poet's mother told her that a strange man was sitting next to her on the couch and then handed the phone to the strange man who was, in actuality, the Alaskan Poet's father. Can't construct a narrative around the Idaho Playwright's father who languished for eight—or was it ten—years in a nursing home, not recognizing anyone but not dead either, caught in some liminal space of which I cannot even begin to conceive. Same thing for my friend Carol's father (some people just don't have nicknames, folks)—every day for twelve years Carol's mother, Fay, visited her Saul at lunchtime, and in the end, he had no idea who she was. But she still went to the nursing home because for better and worse. A lot, lot worse.

I can't make meaning out of why my mom has suffered silently for years, slipping up here and there but really going downhill after my dad died. I don't understand why she has worried her entire life about Alzheimer's, like she's had a premonition. She watched my great-aunt Grace—we called her Dacie, the beginning of nicknames comes two generations before me—struggle at age fifty-four with early-onset Alzheimer's (just three years older than I am now). Dacie was an executive at Dayton's Minneapolis back in the day when Dayton's really was something—the biggest, most elegant department store in Minneapolis. But she had to quit because she couldn't remember how to do her job. My mom was a teenager then and saw all this. Maybe it scared her. Maybe that explains why she quit drinking tea when I was a teenager—because studies linked tea to Alzheimer's. She quit using aluminum pans for a while too. But she was too frugal to go buy anything new, so that didn't last and she began again using the same aluminum pans she'd received as a wedding present. Did these pots and pans contribute to her Alzheimer's? I don't know. I cook with Calphalon which is anodized aluminum. I'm scared to Google it.

℘

Right after my father died, I mean, less than a month, I took my mom with me to Ashland with the Opera Singer and her family. I thought it would be good for my mom, which is a terrible way to make a decision, patronizing really, deciding what might be good for someone else. But my whole life I'd heard how my mother wished she'd gone to more live theater, and my whole adult life I'd been living out that dream. And she said yes. There was no reason not to anymore.

It was a Herculean effort to get my mother to the theater on time, to get her to her seat, to get her to the restroom at intermission. To make sure she didn't trip getting into her seat. (This is such a peeve of mine. Stand the hell up, people! Stop thinking you can just turn your legs to the side. Stand up when someone comes down your aisle.

You need the damn exercise anyway!) I had to ensure she'd been to the restroom before the play began too, so she didn't overflow her Depends, had to make sure she was socially cued as to who was who.

I didn't think it was Alzheimer's then. I thought it was grief that kept her from tracking. God knows I couldn't remember the plays, the plots, and all the players on the stage and in the Opera Singer's family the first year we went to Ashland—and here was my mother, less than a month after my dad died, trying to track—who would think it was anything more than the grief of losing a spouse of forty-six years.

The night I am remembering right now, we were seeing *Twelfth Night*, outside in the Elizabethan Theater. My mother snipped at the Opera Singer. Her sharp tongue admonished the Singer to not touch her walker as the Singer helped her navigate the crowd and get to her seat. I didn't hear it. I can't remember where I was, but if I had to guess, I was in line renting cushions and blankets so that once the sun dropped, we'd be comfortable. Enabling like a good adult child of an alcoholic, you might say. Or, you might say, managing the situation so that my own stress level didn't climb any higher. At any rate, the Opera Singer got my mom situated, while I pushed through the crowd with navy blue polar fleece blankets, cobalt blue pillows, and a bag of Werther's Originals.

My mom and I sat alone, away from the clan of the Opera Singer. Good seats, really, right above the vomitorium, close to stage left. As the play began, my mother reached over and patted and squeezed my right hand, then let her hand linger there. Looking at this now, I see she was apologizing and thanking me in the same move. But all I felt was discomfort. My mother's hand on mine, me standing in as spouse like I had done so many times before. I never wanted this role. Now here I was starring in it. I withdrew into myself. My mother felt it and pulled her hand away.

It was June and hot enough that we didn't need the blankets, and late enough that, as the third act began, the sky was an inky periwinkle blue of deep twilight. The Elizabethan is a replica of the Globe Theater, and when a show is playing, a flag flies from the top of the penthouse, fifty-five feet above the stage. The flag is lit from below and bats and swallows swoop and dip up there, catching the insects attracted to the light. I know now that my mother couldn't track the play. I'd been to *Hamlet* earlier in the week, but my mom stayed in the hotel. Sleeping, crying, sitting catatonic, doing all of these things, I'm sure. And unlike my mother, I'd also seen enough Shakespeare that my ear was attuned to the iambic pentameter, and I could follow the play.

Who knows what my mom thought. She let the words wash over her, and maybe they got in. It doesn't really matter. She got to experience seeing actors on all three levels of the stage and standing on top of the vomitorium nearest us. She thrilled to the trumpets at the beginning of the first and third acts. And she stared in wonder at the bats and swallows, at their graceful acrobatics, at the way they were lit from the stage below and backlit against the rising dark. I watched her watch them, watched the delight and surprise on her face when she noticed them—(and was that Venus shining over stage right?)—a show within a show.

She clasped my hand again, and this time I didn't pull away energetically. I leaned in, literally touching my head to hers. I think she whispered, "Katie, look at the birds! They're magic."

Even that night, though, I remembered a photograph I had of Dacie. Someone had snapped a picture of her from behind as she was standing on a beach in Galveston, Texas, a place she loved for the warm gulf water and the plethora of shorebirds. In the photo, her head is tilted back, lifted toward a great jumble of peach and blue sunset-colored clouds. You can't see her face, but I imagine it has the same look of awe and joy on it that my mother's had when looking up at the birds in the Elizabethan Theater. It's the gift of Alzheimer's, this joy of the ever present, this great tumbling into the now.

I think I knew then. I think I knew but didn't want to know. No one wants their mom to lose her mind. No one wants to think their mother might one day not know them. So, instead, I sat in that dark theater with my mom, and I let her warm hand rest on mine as long as she wanted it to, without it meaning anything more than a gesture of love.

LIFESAVING

My sisters and I laugh. And in these situations, it's all you can do, really. We laugh at the droll, and we laugh at the inane. We laugh at some of my mother's crazy caregivers, and we laugh at the dark. Because if we don't laugh at—and in—the dark, we'll go mad.

Today Sue and I went and looked at an AFH. This is not a partial abbreviation for *America's Funniest Home Videos*. It stands for adult foster home. This is a home of five to eight people who are all waiting to die. Some people live in foster homes for years, but most have a length of stay of less than a year. Foster homes cost the same as assisted living but deliver a much higher level of care. And like a college dorm, you're stuck with who you're stuck with. This worries us for our mother.

Also, we're making the choice to constrain her life more. We moved her from a 2,800-square-foot house to a 550-square-foot apartment in an assisted living facility to an 11-by-11-foot room in a house that she must share with Ben, Leo, JoJo, and Marguerite. The first move was devastating for her cognition, and we were hoping to avoid the second move until she was so far gone that she didn't necessarily register the transition.

This was, unfortunately, not to be.

My mother can't have an MRI, and there's really no reason anyway for someone who is dying to have that procedure just to help her kids try to make sense of what's happening inside her head. The working theory is that, in addition to Alzheimer's, she is having transitory ischemic attacks or TIAs, tiny little strokes, clots, that get jammed up in some brain pathway before shooting their way out and on to—well, I don't know where. The little strokes my mom is having are only going to continue. Physically, she's bounced back from her most recent one and is again walking and getting in and out of bed by herself. But, mentally, this one compromised her demented brain more. While she could probably stay in assisted living another month or two, this day is inevitable. And this foster home specializes in memory care and will take her cat, Sweet Pea—or the Pea in the parlance of my family. This is crucial because those two are so bonded.

I think this decision would be easier if my sister and I had kids. We'd have the experience of sending our kids to school or to camp or on a date—or anywhere, really. My friend, the Tines, who homeschooled her boys until junior high, said to me last night, "It's no different than sending your kid to public school for the first time—with a Mohawk because you slipped with the clippers when you were cutting his hair. You just have to send them out into the world and hope for the best. It's their journey, not yours."

And that's the thing. It's her journey. We have to let her walk it, right? I love the Mary Oliver poem, "The Journey." Its sentiment reminds me of the grace in letting go in these situations and reminds me also that my mom is on her own path, that we are just serving as way finders for her. At the end of her poem, Oliver says, "Determined to do/the only thing you could do—/determined to save/the only life you could save." My sisters and I remind each other that we must let whatever happens to our mother simply occur because it's her journey. Like the Tines with her boys, we're hoping for the best.

NEGRONI (PRN)

I'm not sure which is harder: moving my mom to an adult foster home on the down-low so she wouldn't continually be retraumatized when we had to keep telling her about it, or leaving her there. Which is why tonight I'm sitting at my new favorite restaurant and drinking a Negroni. I ate here two weeks ago tonight with my mom. I feel like I've been in one of those Progressive Insurance "Life Comes at You Fast" commercials. Was it really only two weeks ago that I had this same drink at this same table with my mom?

THE ONLY LIFE YOU CAN SAVE

The same wise therapist who offered me stories in lieu of advice also routinely told me, "The only life you can save is your own." This was a tough lesson for me, *is* a tough sentiment that I have to revisit again and again.

I first got this lesson nine years ago when my mom had a heart attack and open-heart surgery, and my father was largely absent from the scene and abdicated responsibility for care of his wife—my mother—to my sisters and me. At the time, I had the financial resources and the support of my amazing wife so I didn't work for sixteen weeks while I cared for my mom—sitting by her ICU bedside, overseeing her care in the skilled nursing facility, changing her dressings when she lived with my wife and me.

I was killing myself—and, in some respects, my marriage—by trying to save my mother's life. There were all sorts of reasons for this that are fodder for another essay, another book, really. But suffice it to say that something would unhinge my sister Sue or me and then we'd recognize our over-compensating and call the other. Whoever called would barely wait for the "Hello" before blurting, "Say it! Say it to me." And the person who answered the phone would say, "The only life you can save is your own." Then the caller would always exhale a huge breath and usually start crying, and the person on the other end would say as gently and fiercely as possible, "The *only* life you can save is your *own.*"

That advice has stood me in good stead in many situations. In uneven relationships. In caregiving. In truly dangerous situations like earthquakes and falling out of a kayak in cold, cold water. But today and yesterday, I've been chanting it over and over to remind myself to leave my mother's bedside as she slides inexorably and excruciatingly slowly toward death. I remember that sitting there with her or doing just one more thing to make her comfortable will neither prevent nor hasten her death, but it may indeed speed mine.

And so I go to my home at a reasonable hour and take a bath and get into bed even though sleep doesn't come. I stop to wash my dishes before rushing out in the morning. I make a green smoothie of spinach, beets, and celery so that I'll have some healthy food. I don't get to the gym, but all the lifting I'm doing of my mother assures a good lower body workout.

My mother may die tonight. Or next week. Or in three weeks. Or in three months. The timeline isn't clear, but we are in the window. It's sad because it's, well, sad, and because it's my mom, and it's the end. But we are born alone and die alone. No one can do that work for us. So I'm home tonight, writing this to you out there because the only life you can save is your own.

HERE/THERE, BOTH/AND

The thing about death is that it's incredibly paradoxical. Because someone is dying, your energy is focused solely on the present moment. Everything falls away, and you are unaware of time passing or hunger. You only know the rising and falling of your own breath and the breath of the dying person.

Also because a person is dying, everything feels like a huge fucking emergency. Why is that brown Camry torturing me by driving two miles per hour under the speed limit? Why did the Union Cab taxi dispatcher take thirty minutes to call me back to tell me the cab wasn't coming? Why! Is! The! God! Damned! Internet! So! Slow! I mean, it's practically running at dial-up speeds. Gawd! It's like your system gets overtaxed and the synapses can only spend so long vibrating at the intense frequency that is the death energy. Too much time there—not enough time in nature or at the gym or quietly chopping vegetables—and the nerve endings start to feel like even the line in Starbucks is too much. (Or maybe just the third triple tall, one-third decaf Americano is too much.)

When my mom was sick the first time and we thought then that she would die, I didn't understand this. I didn't understand how the liminal space that the dying person is in can affect your own psyche. And so sometimes I would leave the ICU of the hospital in Tacoma and drive back to Portland and have no idea how I got there. One time, I looked up and out, as if seeing the road for the first time. This was right around Castle Rock, where I-5 starts to climb toward Kelso and Longview. The light had this blue-green quality. It was late dusk, and the Doug Firs were pressing in on the freeway, and there was a distinct lack of traffic driving north. And I remember not knowing if I was on US 101 near San Anselmo or on I-5. I mean, I *truly* didn't know. Joe Cocker was singing his rendition of "Bye Bye Blackbird" or maybe Van Morrison was singing "Tupelo Honey." I am not entirely sure, but I know the music was old enough to have been getting radio play on KMEL, the classic rock station I listened to when I was twenty-something and prone to driving around Marin County late at night. And I felt then—that night I drove from Tacoma to Portland and didn't know if I'd see my mom alive again—like I had felt in my twenties. Lost. Confused. Disoriented. Was I twenty-one or forty-one? Was I here or there?

I love this paragraph by Courtney E. Martin:

> It's tempting to live a life where you only show up in public once you've stitched yourself back together again. It's so much easier to acknowledge pain once you have a pat story about the meaning that's been wrought, the silver lining that's been carefully drawn. But it's not honest. Rituals are so powerful because they provide structure for the full spectrum of our emotional lives: the births and the deaths, the union and the disintegration. Without them, we live a few octaves short.

Everything is always both/and, isn't it? We are alive, and we are dying. We are there, and we are here. We are confused, and in our confusion we are finally able to see clearly and sing out in our full range.

WHAT WE DON'T KNOW

This week in Portland there were several days over ninety-five degrees and one day it was one hundred degrees. In the Pacific Northwest, this is akin to burning in a lake of fire. We don't really know what to do *with* this weather, *in* this weather. So far, we've had twenty-seven days of weather at ninety degrees or higher. I spent the entire week driving around in the Ironman's two-door Ford Ranger manual with a bench seat and no air conditioning. While I was grateful for the second vehicle—especially one that could haul some shit—it was a challenge to drive around in the heat and traffic, windows down, and clutch in (and out, and in and out).

At one point, I was driving across town from St. John's to Gateway and on the off-ramp from I-84, a guy in an air-conditioned pickup from some electric company cut me off. I let him. I did not gesticulate, but I did swear loudly and profusely. He couldn't hear me. His windows were rolled up and the Freon was keeping him cool. Then his finger came out the window, and the man who had just cut me off flipped me the bird. The man who cut me off! As we came to the stoplight at the top of the off-ramp, he also stuck his camera phone out the window and took a picture of me and my vehicle. To intimidate me, I guess.

I came unhinged. I flipped him off. Multiple times. I gesticulated wildly. I shouted. I pretended to take a picture of his commercial vehicle.

Then he got out of his car and started walking toward me. I thought, "I hope that motherfucker hits me so that I can sue him." I was that unhinged. The heat, the near-death of everything, the days and days of getting up at 5:45 and into my office by 6:30 so that I could meet both client and familial obligations—all of it conspired to make me wish for a nice old-fashioned fist fight.

My kind mentor tells me that there are really very few instances of true anger. She says at the root of it usually there are four or five emotions: fear, shame, sadness, love, (and maybe) surprise. I don't like to admit she's right very often, but when I reflect on this situation now, I can see that at the root of all this wild hand waving and swearing was fear and sadness and tiredness. My mom was dying, and I was afraid and sad for her, for me, for my family.

I suppose I was also afraid of this hulking mass of an electrician who swaggered toward me in his mustard-colored, double-front Carhartts. But the thing is, when you are driving a truck without a radio, air conditioning, or power steering, you are also driving a truck without electric windows. There was no way I could get my window rolled up before he reached me.

He got right up in my face and said "Why are you waving your arms so much? What's the matter with you?" I explained—calmly, in fact—his various infractions, including flipping me off. He laughed and said, "I guess that was stupid of me." I started to cry. I said, "You have no idea what another person is going through." I told him about my mom. He took my hand. Right through the window of the truck, he held my hand and said, "I'm sorry. I just had a huge rolling brownout in downtown, and I was crazed too. I love you, sister."

I apologized too. He walked back to his truck, and I thought about all the ways that exchange could have gone—from fists to pistols. I was grateful for the moment of grace, for the way total strangers could forgive and care for each other. If I were going to give advice to myself last week, I'd say, "Dear stressed-out fifty-year-old, don't ignore improbable moments of grace and stay stuck in the mire of your story. Also, remember that *everyone* is telling themselves a story. And nobody really knows what the hell they're doing. We're all just muddling through the best we can."

DEATH IS LIKE THIS

Death is like this: it's exhausting is what it is. It's sitting at your kitchen table at 6:30 a.m. because you can't sleep. Your middle sister, Sue, is propped up on one elbow, sprawled across your Ikea sleeper sofa, her makeup from the day before streaked across her cheeks, skin showing through in the spots where her CPAP mask rubbed off the carefully layered foundation of vitamin C serum, BB cream, Bare Minerals, and blush. Eyes clumpy with mascara as much from lack of sleep as from crying all the way to your house after you left your mother unconscious at the care facility.

Death is like this: two sisters drinking a pot of coffee at 6:30 in the morning, and one saying to the other, "Kate, we've got to get $15,000 out of mom's checking account before the Feds notify the bank that she's dead."

And you, crying, resigned that even in this moment you're not allowed a full emotional response, even when you know today is the day your mom is going to die. You get up and write a check to yourself, sign it yourself, and put it under your phone so you don't forget to deposit it in your own bank account. Death is like this: nothing but business details and the weirdness of being the attorney in fact when you should be grieving.

And then your other sister, Jule, is calling, saying, "She's dead, she's gone. I was only asleep for a minute, I swear. But she's dead."

And you and Sue look at each other and exhale huge breaths and gulp your coffee and grab keys and purses— well, okay, it's Sue who grabs a gigantic Dolce & Gabbana purse, you just grab a wallet—and you also take the half-gallon mason jar of green smoothie that your ex-ex-girlfriend made for you and put in the refrigerator two days earlier for this moment when time is telescoping and collapsing at once, and you pour the last of the coffee into a cup that you and your sister will share in the car on the drive across town. And you pick up your phone and the check and you deposit it in the ATM and thank god that your mother had the good sense to die on a Saturday so that maybe the deposit will go through first thing Monday morning, leaving you some working capital to manage all the costs that you know come with death—and finally when the machine has sucked in the check and spit out the card and you are heading east on Lombard, crossing the cut out of St. John's, you turn to Sue and say, "Do you think she was gasping? Do you think Jule gave her enough morphine? Do you think she knew we loved her?" And here you start to cry because death is like this.

And then you are at the adult foster home, and there is Jule, and she is keening on your shoulder, keening in this high-pitched wail of unadulterated grief, saying she's sorry she fell asleep—and not letting you yet touch your mother because you are comforting your sister. You are the paterfamilias now, comforting your sister like the head of household. When you finally disentangle from her, you wail over your mother's dead body, so small in the bed, still so hot, still burning with the fever of the dehydrated—she's not been dead that long—feeling her soft belly, noticing how it no longer rises and falls, and you want just one more moment with this vessel that bore you before you have to assume the role, and sign the paperwork, and move forward because death is like this.

II.

Fall

DEAR MOM

For the first time in fifteen years I'm not cooking a Thanksgiving feast for you and Dad. No organic, heritage breed, million-dollar bird brining in the fridge. No gluten-free stuffing soaking up butter and broth in the big stockpot, the one usually reserved for cooking Chinese herbs. On the counter there are no bags of chanterelle mushrooms stuck with Doug Fir needles and soil from the forest floor. No white cremini mushrooms that look as scrubbed as choirboys, or the cipollini onions that take so long to peel and boil but are so worth it when added to the mushrooms and butter. The clear butter cubby on the refrigerator door sits empty too—I mean, unless you count the wasabi paste and one of your old insulin syringes in there.

When we were kids, we'd follow you around Roger Wilco and Alpha Beta, and later, in high school, we'd follow you through the Safeway that finally came to town. We'd watch you throw the yellow boxes of Kellogg's brand cubed stuffing into the basket, cans of Ocean Spray jellied cranberry sauce, a bottle of Kitchen Bouquet (because god forbid the gravy shouldn't be a deep mahogany; you led us to believe white gravy was not only unappetizing but unpalatable as well), decorative squash for a centerpiece, canned yams in heavy syrup for your sweet potatoes (topped with marshmallows to complete the diabetic delight), ten pounds of russet potatoes, and the frozen bird.

No heritage bird, yours. Norbest or Butterball at seventeen cents a pound or free if you bought a hundred dollars' worth of groceries. And you always did—especially after you added cans of green and black olives, jars of spiced apple rings, sweet gherkins, and mini dills for the relish trays, plus mixed nuts for the sterling silver nut cups. (The same ones your ungrateful children sold in the estate sale, because ever since all the good help went away in the war, we just couldn't imagine ourselves polishing eighteen silver nut cups for the three high holy meals we eat each year.)

Here's what I loved about your Thanksgiving: the turkey floating in the bathtub, as it finished defrosting. Did it bob there overnight? Or for just a few hours in the morning as you made the dressing, the mashed potatoes, and the creamed onions that only landed gentry had a taste for? In Minnesota, I remember stuffing the bird the night before, putting it in a disposable roasting pan, covering it all with aluminum foil, and then setting it in the trunk of your car. I'm pretty sure global warming and fear of foodborne illness has ruined that trick, though.

I also remember the year you fell prey to marketing and bought a bird with a pop-up plastic timer embedded in the breast. The side dishes sat in the second wall oven, the onions bubbled gently in their chafing dish as the Sterno kept them warm, and the turkey—well, the bird continued cooking because the timer had not yet popped. You were in your blue chambray dress, a scarf nattily knotted at the neck. You leaned an elbow on the mantle and sipped your second scotch and water—maybe your third—and you wept. Because the turkey. The meal. The symbolism. The reality.

These are the nostalgic memories. The Norman Rockwell holiday memories we're "supposed" to have. The darker memories exist, as well, and I wouldn't be me and this wouldn't be the *Authenticity Experiment* if I didn't mention the number of times I counted how many glasses of wine my dad drank or remembered the time my ex-wife and I did dishes simply so we could finish the remainder of everyone else's wine, along with the rest of the bottle. Because let's not lie, these dinners were equal parts big laughter and big tension. At some point, you always were in the back bathroom crying or out on the patio smoking a cigarette and cooling off.

Even last year, your last Thanksgiving. You got mad at me instead of my dad because he had the gall to die before you. It was your Alzheimer's-riddled brain that did it. But you were so mad, and it took so much effort to calm you down, and of course, that is what I hold on to. Not you, sitting at the counter in the Tines's kitchen, drinking wine and laughing. Instead I remember standing at the foot of your bed, after I'd driven you home in absolute silence, and telling you I didn't know if this would be your last Thanksgiving, that I just wanted a nice evening and I didn't know why you were so angry.

Do you remember what you said to me? You said, "I don't know why I do this. It's like there's something wrong with my brain. I don't even know why I'm mad. And why at you, who always tries so hard?" I figured explaining about the Alzheimer's brain didn't make sense at this point. Grief overtook you, and so I held your hand while we both cried.

This year, before dinner, I'll go for a ride, just like I've done for the past six years. It's supposed to be in the low forties, and so I'll wear my secret wool shirt and long-sleeved jersey, my fleece-lined tights, and my neoprene shoe covers. It may even be cold enough for the lobster-claw gloves. Under my helmet, I'll have on the black skull cap you think makes me look like a serial killer—although to be fair, you think that about most caps, and you're wrong.

I have a bit of magical thinking around you and dad now, imagining you watching me ride, really seeing what an athlete I am. That's the great thing about death, I suppose,

THE HISTORY IN THE CHIMNEY
OF MY HEART

For the last two weekends I've ridden ferries across Puget Sound. The day after Thanksgiving, I drove my alien green Kia Soul onto the MV *Chetzemoka* and crossed from Point Defiance in Tacoma to the Tahlequah ferry dock on Vashon Island.

The ferry sailed toward the far shore, and the clear, cold air bit my cheeks as I stood on the bow of the car deck and watched the crazy Sufi dance of sunlight play off the dark gray sound. I sipped from a cup of coffee mixed with hot chocolate and watched Vashon come closer, closer and felt such a sharp memory: thirty years earlier, maybe more, a warm May day, sailing to the island with my wife. (Although she wasn't my wife then. Well, she was, but I couldn't say that word then—my psyche, the culture, neither would allow it.)

But that's what we were, each other's spouses. And we were sailing to Vashon, maybe even on the same ferry, although back then we drove my burgundy Volvo 245 DL onboard, for a dinner at Sound Food. The world stretched out before us in that way it does when you are only nineteen or twenty. All the potential and possibility still there. Do you remember how that was? How you thought you could do anything? Become anyone? I think that is what I loved most about that life and that wife—that we continually remade ourselves. Partially it's a factor of being so young when we fell in love, partially it's who we were together.

But maybe I am not remembering this right. Maybe it was me who was continually dreaming. A short story writer who could drink water glasses of gin without repercussions and somehow magically afford a Victorian resplendent with Turkish carpets and tobacco-brown leather club chairs. A reporter for the *Wall Street Journal* on assignment in Paris, living in a glass-walled loft and drinking red wine late into the night at some bistro. A novelist living at Salmon Beach in some shabby chic shack and subsisting on sourdough bread, Dungeness crab, and Semillon blanc. And in every world, my wife.

The quantum streams had not yet narrowed, and we talked into the early morning hours imagining where we might end up, and how. It never occurred to me that my dreams might not be hers—because when you are nineteen and twenty and twenty-one, you are undifferentiated from anyone you love. Undifferentiated maybe in the best sense. In the sense that makes for cheesy pop music and tragic breakup songs. If we never fell in love in our early twenties, the music industry would simply shut down.

But we do fall in love. And the great joy of being in love in your twenties is discovering the world together. If you had asked me before I drove my Kia Soul onto the ferry some of the worlds my wife and I had discovered together, I'd have remembered the meal at Sound Food, the warm May night, the air moist and briny and pungent with Puget Sound. I'd have remembered the mixed greens and homemade bread. And I'd have remembered the sense of possibility I felt. But it would not have been until my fifty-year-old self was driving along Quartermaster Harbor Road and passed a sign that said, "Roadside Attraction" that I would have remembered the delight we felt reading Tom Robbins's *Another Roadside Attraction*, or how all the books our young minds devoured fed the potential we saw for our lives and helped us to differentiate from our parents, as we grew closer together as a couple.

People wonder what it was like to be young and in

love and closeted. And I think, perhaps, that's why my wife and I were so bonded, so enmeshed. Because that's all we had, each other. The culture and our families certainly weren't celebrating us. In 1985 gay bars—even in big cities like Seattle—still didn't have many windows, and you found them down side streets and alleys. And that is where you found us congregating. Gay student unions weren't prevalent yet. Parades were full of leathermen and dykes on bikes and not the ally groups you see today. PFLAG had only gone national in 1980. We had only each other—queers and outcasts, all of us—and that is, maybe, what made our lives so entwined and why I am now loathe to let go of my ex-wife, because she is *my* history. We are *each other's* history.

Or maybe none of this is true. Maybe all I felt as I drove through that brilliant sunshine toward Southwest Seventy-Fifth Avenue and the chaotic home of my adopted family and a dinner of pork roast with white beans and polenta was a wave of nostalgia for a ferry ride and a book I read a long time ago. Two things that Tom Robbins said "built their nests in the chimney of my heart."

BECAUSE DEATH

I have a picture of my three sisters: Jule, Sue, and Sue's wife, Jen, who is as much my sister as any blood relation. We are in Minneapolis, memorialized in black and white after our mother's own memorial earlier in the afternoon. We've all been drinking, because death.

I love this picture, and I look at it daily because it calls up the feelings of protection and unconditional love I have for my family. How I will kill the fool that hurts them. How, the minute my mother died, I suddenly felt the need to buy a big house, a house with enough bedrooms for everyone, a formal dining room with seating for twenty so that I could fit my blood family and my chosen family, a family room with a big-screen television and two hundred channels of cable for my sisters who love their shows: *Design on a Dime*, *American Horror Story*, *Chopped*, and fifteen other shows I have no idea about but primarily involve home decorating or mysterious violence (neither of which I can really abide), and a basement office for me where I could sequester myself and work or just take a deep breath and be my introverted self.

In this picture of my family, I look protective, my arms are stretched as wide as Jesus on the cross, reaching to pull my three sisters toward me, like we are one. Yet, perhaps it's also true that I am different from the rest of them. My mother used to bristle when I'd ask her to turn down the television, playing at two hundred decibels, saying, "Are you really my child? You live a quiet, dull, controlled life." And I'd think, *Fuck you, the chaos is not helping your confusion.*

Or perhaps I am not different at all. Picture our mother dying, slowly, over twenty days in August. Picture

Sue staying with me. Picture the lists, the tasks, the frangible balancing act of caregiving and managing both our day jobs. Picture all the stacks of mail and activities of daily living pushed aside, including the weekly box of organic vegetables just sitting on the counter. Then picture Sue saying, "Kate, I was gonna put your farm box of vegetables in the refrigerator, but I knew you'd freak out if I messed up your system."

I laughed. "I don't have a system."

"It's not exactly a system," she said, her tone rising along with her eyebrow, the slyest of smiles playing out on her lips. "It's more like OCD."

Sue has OCD tendencies. When she was a kid, we just called it "her germ." As in, "Sue has to get her germ before we can go." Her germ could have been the particular way she touched the light switch. The way she wrapped her hand around the doorknob before she left the house. The way she put on her socks and shoes. It was no big deal. Not pathologized by any of us—parents, siblings, or the kids in the neighborhood. I remember this one time there was a gaggle of neighborhood kids in the house, and Sue kept swiping her hand around and around the bathroom light switch, and someone new asked what the delay was. The boy who lived across the street held up his hand and said, "Just a minute. Sue's getting her germ." No weirdness whatsoever. Just Sue being Sue.

Picture my face when Sue said, "It's more like OCD." I immediately went all Monk and felt worried. But I laughed simultaneously because, well, my refrigerator is like a filing cabinet. Leafy greens in the right drawer—always— along with semi-hard veggies like cucumbers and zucchini. Root vegetables and celery (which is usually used with root veggies) in the left drawer. Corn sort of confounds me. It's not a root vegetable, but you have to peel it to get to the goods, so it's in the root vegetable drawer too. Cabbage and lettuce in bags at the back of lowest shelf. I could continue, but you get the point. (I justify my refrigerator as an antidote to the insanely discombobulated refrigerator I grew up with.)

But I digress. Return to the picture of my arms around my siblings and the house I dream for us. Then picture me looking at Redfin every day. Really, every single day. At all the houses I could afford if I was willing to work harder. This isn't any judgment or perfectionism on my part. I'm simply not willing to work—let's tell the truth, I am constitutionally incapable of working—forty hours a week in an office, and so the house I dream of for my family is just that, a dream. The reality is also that I would spend fifty weeks a year knocking around in that big house by myself. Because my sisters haven't been here since my mom died, even though we all thought we'd spend more time together after she died. We haven't. Because life goes on the way it always has.

But I am the paterfamilias still. So much so that I had my father's tuxedos tailored to fit me and then wore the black tux to a photo shoot for new headshots. Sue called me after I sent her the pictures. She may have been crying a little. She said, "These pictures are so great, Kate, because you're so you—you've made Dad's suit your own, you're wearing his watch. You've literally made yourself into the head of our family, and you look like it."

I suppose in some ways I always was.

WITNESS

This morning the Alaskan Poet arrived. Although she'd flown all night and slept very little, we sat at the quarter-sawn oak kitchen table and drank coffee and talked.

This table has sat in my dining room ever since we moved my mother to assisted living. Before that, it was in my parents' great room in Sequim, and before that, in the breakfast room of the house I grew up in. Earlier still, the table—at that point varnished in an ugly olive green stain that chipped easily and exposed the oak below—was unused, relegated to a basement corner of my paternal grandparents' Milwaukee, Wisconsin, home.

For most of my life, I've heard the squeaks and creaks of this wood table and its matching chairs, and when they finally arrived, I felt confused when I heard those sounds in my own house, by which I mean the grownup adult-self house that I own alone. During the quiet morning hours when I would sit at this table and work on the essays that were to become *Objects In Mirror Are Closer Than They Appear,* it made me profoundly uncomfortable to hear a sound I associated with my father shifting in his chair. It was like a lightning strike to my psyche, and one morning I snapped and frantically Googled "Furniture repair, restoration, Portland, OR." As with so many Google searches, I got the information, sent some emails, and went no further.

This morning, as the Poet and I sat at the table talking about our mother's similarities, the Poet's new manuscript, and the devastation of watching someone lose themselves day by day and the pain of our own loss in that process, I looked at the two coffee cups sitting on coasters on the table. We were both comfortable and engaged, leaning back in our chairs. The chairs squeaked and creaked when we shifted our weight, and when one of us rested elbows on the table, it made noise too. But the noise didn't grate on my nerves as usual. There was something lovely in this moment of the table's continuity, in the fact that the Poet and I were memorializing the best of our mothers in this conversation and in our work, that we could laugh and shake our heads about the bad without a hint of bitterness, and laugh darkly about it too. And that the table stood there to witness it all.

I KNEW I KNEW WHAT I KNEW

Today would have been the seventy-fourth birthday of my mentor, friend, and editor. She died last year on November 6 after living years with cancer. I say "living years" rather than "battling cancer" or "courageously fighting cancer" because Judith Kitchen would not cotton to those ideas. Nor would she like the soft language of "passed away" or "crossed over." Judith Kitchen, daughter of a scientist, very much a father's daughter, demanded specificity in all things—especially language. Ergo, she died. She is dead.

But seventy-two years ago, she was a toddler speaking her first sentence, "My do it." Anyone who knew Judith is not surprised by this sentence. I've never met someone who knew her own mind more than Judith. Her husband, Stan, once told me that Judith could fall asleep at midnight and wake up the next morning and continue talking *at* Stan about the very subject on which she had been expounding eight hours earlier.

Judith had reason to talk so much, to share her ideas with anyone who would listen. Because for years, like so many women of her generation, she was silenced. This is from her essay "Mending Wall," which ran in *Seneca Review*.

> "Too bad," said my wonderful professor, "that you have so many good ideas, and no vehicle with which to express them." Well, I had a vehicle, but it just wasn't the one he recognized—the language of the scholarly article. It just didn't dot the i's or cross the t's or proceed logically on its way to its point. It circled and spiraled; it doubled back; it digressed and prodded; it spoke in tongues. And yet I knew I knew

what I knew—knew it in ways that, if I thought to remember, sounded a bit like my father's way of knowing something that he then had to prove. But since there is no such thing as "proof" in literature, it seemed to me that all I had to do was find a way to show the direction of my thoughts. Demonstrate them. Point the reader toward my inconclusive conclusions.

That was 1962. It took more than a quarter of a century for me to discover that, yes, you could simply put your feet on the desk and think on the page. You could let your thoughts float out—in their incomplete sentences, their sinuous meanderings—and maybe, sometimes, they would find a way to coalesce and become a larger thought, a meaning.

Judith was never bitter that she had to wait all those years to find the right vehicle for her words, wait longer still for recognition. And recognized she was. She won the Anhinga Prize in poetry, two Pushcart Prizes for essay, the Lillian Fairchild Award for her novel *The House on Eccles Road*, and an NEA fellowship. Before she died, Judith was called one of the three most influential poetry critics in the United States.

Judith and I often talked about the writer's persona and the projections readers place on all writers, but especially writers of nonfiction. We told each other about the stories we'd written that shocked readers and why we'd written those instead of the other, more painful ones. Lauded for our honesty, we both admitted that there were several stories we could not approach, even in fiction. Every writer has her limits.

I have a broadside of Judith's poem "Perennials," which is the title poem for her collection that won the Anhinga Prize. It hangs in my dining room, above the table where I write. I love to imagine the amused eye of JK looking down on me from that spot. This morning when I came downstairs, the broadside was crooked on the wall. I'm sure it could happen. I probably bumped it when I opened the dining room window. But I've been opening and closing the window all year, and this is the first time the picture has been askew. Judith would hate that I ascribed meaning to what was clearly—surely must have been—a random act. Her science brain could not broach sentimentality or New Age spirituality. That's okay. I choose to believe I'm getting the last laugh, as Judith has discovered that quantum physics is right and her energy is everywhere, including here this morning in my dining room.

GRIEF DISPATCHES

My sister Sue has always called this blog The Authenticity Report. Partly because she got the name wrong the first time she heard it, and partly because she thinks of these essays as dispatches from the field. Sue's voice is in my head a lot lately. It makes sense given the year we had and the things we accomplished—like finding our mom a good place to die and moving her there in the span of seven days—and then sitting with her the three days it took her to die. But also Sue's voice is in my head because I think she is funny and smart and more judgmental than I am. She has a kind of pragmatic judgment that I'm often lacking. Sue will not take any shit from anyone anytime. Just ask her wife or our little sister, Jule.

I called Sue recently, on the floor about my latest losses, one of which is my cat, the Pea. I inherited our mother's cat. And it is no surprise, really, but it *is* a bit uncanny that the cat is quite suddenly dying of congestive heart failure and kidney failure—the things listed on our mother's death certificate—and also of cancer, which is what killed our father. Sue and I were discussing cat oncologists, how unfair and strange it is that I am managing another project of our parents, the cost of vet care, the reality of life-prolonging treatments. I mean, do you pay $10,000 so your mother's cat doesn't die within six months of her and you don't flip the fuck out? Or do you let the cat die and pay $10,000 in extra therapy because the cat died within six months of your mother? It's a real question.

Our dad's dog died three months to the day after our dad did, so the cat's scenario isn't really that shocking. But after almost nine years without my own animal, I love having the Pea—love sitting on the couch at night and holding her, talking to her about my day (you know, like she cares). I like telling her the story of her life. I say, "First you were an abandoned stray in the Rainbow's End trailer park that backed up to the 101 freeway, and some kind lady put food out for you so you didn't die until the Humane Society could capture you. Then your old daddy and old mama rescued you and brought you to their house. Then your dad died, then both your dogs died, and then you had to move with your mama to Portland, Oregon. Then that mama died, and now I'm your new mama." And I swear to you, every single time I recite this story to that cat, she mews at the end of it. Yes. She mews. Like she understands every word.

Who knows why these losses—in my life, in my sisters' lives, in the Pea's life, in your life—who knows why they have come in such a cluster. They have. They do. They will continue to do so because that's life, right? And all we can do is let go and let the river carry us, because if you fight the current, you will drown. Maybe not immediately. Maybe not for twenty years. But you'll drown nevertheless. I know it because I've seen it happen. More than once.

A woman recently sent me one of my favorite poems by Gregory Orr. Orr, you may know, accidentally killed his brother in a hunting accident, and if he can go on from that, we all can. So take a deep breath and dive in. It is better downstream, I'm sure of it.

> Grief will come to you.
> Grip and cling all you want,
> It makes no difference.
> Catastrophe? It's just waiting to happen.
> Loss? You can be certain of it.
> Flow and swirl of the world.
> Carried along as if by a dark current.

TORNADO WEATHER

This week I ate at The Observatory on Southeast Stark Street. It was Stef's favorite restaurant even though it was loud and hard to have an intimate conversation. She loved their burgers and I loved their BBQ shrimp appetizer. We'd sit in this little corner of the bar, backs to the front door (first to be shot in a raid), in the short seats no one ever wanted, and we'd lean our heads together and talk.

We first ate there in July of 2012, when I was still drinking and had just rolled back into town after mountain bike camp, and I sucked down the Negronis that the bartender poured exceptionally well. The Opera Singer had left by then, so there was no one to show my very impressive bruises to except Stef, who acted appropriately horrified, especially because she didn't cycle, and so things like the pedal bites in the back of my calves looked really mean and nasty to her. In fact, they were.

We went there for her birthday in October 2014. Probably, honestly, the last time Stef ate out in a restaurant. I brought my mom along because my mom and Stef, they loved each other. You can see it in the pictures I took that night. Their heads are turned toward each other, big smiles across both their faces. Menus confounded my mother, and she wanted me to order her a drink. Stef wanted one too, so like a fool, I got two little old ladies something up in a glass—which you know means it had a lot of alcohol in it. They both got drunk—accidentally—but I think they loved the feeling of being out, surrounded by young hipsters, being buzzed, the restaurant almost shaking with noise. My mother said it reminded her of being in North Beach in the sixties and made her feel young again.

The problem came when we went to leave. My mom

fell. I later learned from a Sunday *New York Times* feature on Alzheimer's that noise and talking while walking exacerbates the Alzheimer's shuffle and makes a person more prone to falling. My mom was talking, and there was noise, and there was a lip to the door, and the light had also changed, and people with Alzheimer's can't see beiges very well, so she likely just didn't see the sidewalk.

She went down, and I couldn't lift her. These Tibetans helped me. They totally lied and said they were nurses. I protested, but the man put his hand on my arm and said, "It's okay. It's okay. Let me help you this one time." And Jesus, it makes me cry even now typing that. I was stone cold then, though. One single tear eking out of my left eye. I just wanted to get her into the car and home.

I felt so much like it was my fault. Like I'd given my kid a sippy cup of rum or something. And I just couldn't deadlift her. I could now—I could deadlift her now that I've been training again. But back then she was on one knee, and her vest had caught on the edge of her walker, and I worried that if I moved her wrong I'd dislocate her replaced hip. And I had been slacking on the strength training, my time taken up with an emotionally demanding girlfriend, my mother's care, and my day job. The Tibetans got on either side of my mother and seemingly levitated her upright and, on either elbow to stabilize her, got her to my dead father's Audi (now driven only by me). They lowered her into the passenger seat.

That *Times* article, it ruined me. All the things I wish I'd known. Some I figured out too late. Like staging my mom's makeup for her because she could no longer discern "If A then B." Once I figured that out and started staging it for her, she could do her makeup almost as fast as ever. I also started laying out her clothes for her. Otherwise, she forgot she had clothes or even where they were. But if I laid them out on her bed, it was like she had magically replenishing clothes. Sometimes I'd come over and she'd say, "Look at this great shirt I found! Did you buy this for me? I love it." And sometimes I would have, and sometimes it was just that I'd put it out for her and, hallelujah, she got dressed and hadn't overflowed her diaper with pee, and she felt like a valuable human. And sometimes even if I had bought the shirt for her, I'd tell her I hadn't, that she had good taste. Geminis love to know they have good taste. Then I'd hand her some earrings and a necklace, and she'd feel normal for a minute, like she had some success dressing herself. Until she forgot again.

In the console of my car, above the radio, I still have three of her lipsticks. I kept them there because she'd lose them, and she always wanted lipstick before even being wheeled into the doctor. And I think because she lost the ability to see color, sometimes she'd use the lipstick as rouge additive. I'd say, "You have on rouge." And she'd say, "Not enough." It was an exercise in my own discomfort, being willing to let her be as she was. Like sending your kid to school on picture day dressed the way they want to dress and not the way you'd want to memorialize first grade. I should get rid of those lipsticks, but they're cheap, and they don't melt, and I'm not quite ready to let them go. Maybe I'll have a ritual on Mother's Day with them.

The day after we three ate at The Observatory, I took Stef to the hospital for the procedure that I believed caused her cancer to grow out of control. And four months after we took these pictures, Stef was dead; six more months and my mom was dead too. Looking now at these pictures feels like the moment right before the tornado touches down. And how truly ironic that the low light and lack of

III.

Winter

INSTRUCTIONS FOR GRIEVING

Look, you know how to do this, you really do. Remember, you've done this two times before, and you know the steps to this dance even though you hate every moment of being on this particular dance floor. Wash your laundry, fold it, put it away. Balance your checkbook. Keep your kitchen clean. Make your bed—every day. Prep your meals on Sunday night. Go to the gym and lift heavy weights and let this grief bubble up and out through your cells. Like it does. Like it has the two other times. Remember that feeling of relief after you deadlift 195 pounds or bench press 100.

Go ride your bike outside. Whether it's raining or not. Ride hard, ride fast, ride slow, but kiddo, go for a ride. And when your brain starts spinning at a faster rpm than your wheels and you are crying and having an argument or a conversation with someone who isn't there, remember then to stop. Stop and notice three things. Saturday, riding out on the island, you saw a dead crane stretched out and flat in the stubble of a muddy winter field, and you thought about death and that it could sometimes be beautiful. You saw the bluest of bluebirds in the trees above the wildlife refuge and you thought about your yurt and how that area is called Bluebird Heaven and how you are never there enough. You saw a baby hawk sitting on a telephone junction box, scowling and trying to look bigger and braver than she felt. Be like that hawk. Act as if.

And then remember your breath—in and out, rising and falling—breath comes in, breath goes out, and emotions pass. Breathe through it: it's three bad minutes, five bad minutes, maybe twenty bad minutes max. Then it's two hours of relief all without the aid of Ativan. Just keep breathing and soon you'll get by with less Ativan than you can imagine. (And just a reminder that also with the breath there are your prayers and the candle that you keep burning on your altar. When has the divine ever failed you? And don't tell me often. Because she hasn't. She isn't. You needed more space to heal and grow and write and now you have it.)

Also, remember you are not fifteen, you are fifty-one. You have a checkbook and keys to a car that you own and a mortgage payment that in six years you have never once been in danger of missing. Oh, and you can buy bourbon legally.

Don't forget your friends. They've circled their wagons of love around you. These friends are fierce and right here in the city, in real life. Dinners, brunches, bike rides, lectures, early morning texts, late night emojis. These guys are here to distract you from your head and your heart, from getting stuck wandering around and around the Elizabeth Kübler-Ross mulberry bush of loss.

And when it all gets to be too much, I want to remind you to curl into a ball on the couch and cry. Let it out so it doesn't get trapped. Remember that on Saturday you thought you were going to die, and just six minutes later you got up and went for a bike ride. Because you can do this. You've totally got this. It's transitory.

I'm not saying that this time won't leave you slightly maimed, that you won't walk with the slightest limp the rest of your life. You probably will. Every time you play "Five Foot Two" on a uke, your chest will constrict a little. Every February 9, May 7, May 22, May 27, August 29, or October 4 you'll note the date and maybe feel a heaviness in your body, or a longing, or just a keen missing for one more conversation. And there will be moments like today in church when that small blonde kid kept worrying her hands over and over—she split your heart right open because of how much she reminded you of the way your own small self sometimes feels when considering all this loss and all the ways that you feel alone in the world (even if you really aren't). And the tears just leaked out of your eyes—but they would have anyways because that's who you are.

One last reminder: the transit of midlife is hard, especially if you're trying to do it with some degree of consciousness. But it is a transit. Liminal. And not without joy. Recall the words of David Steindl-Rast, the Benedictine monk: "Happiness is not steady, but joy can be steady. Joy is the happiness that doesn't depend on what happens." Which is why the cure for a broken heart is always bikes, other butches, friends, organic food, sunlight, the river, and the ability to laugh at yourself. These bring you joy always, which means you can always be happy no matter what happens. I'm just saying.

REMAINS

I spent the afternoon going through dead people's boxes. Let me be clear, these *boxes* did not technically belong to the dead people. Instead they were full of *items* that belonged to the dead people or their children.

In one box sat Stef's purse, which until today I had not been able to tackle. A purse is so, well, personal. And the black leather multi-compartmented bag smelled like her—a mix of leather and breath mints and face powder. (Maybe all late sixty-something's purses smell similar? My mother's purse is—was?—a mix of leather, Kleenex, and lipstick.) Stef's purse held her driver's license—including an expired license with a better picture, taken before Ron's death—her Medicare card, her AARP card, a card from St. Jude Medical that listed the serial number and type of pacemaker installed in her chest, and a card from BioGift, the organization that wouldn't take her body the day she died.

The BioGift card made me laugh out loud. It said, "I'm donating my body to science." And if you are close to my age, you just said what I said out loud to myself, down there in the cold, single-car garage. You said, "Science!" (As in, "She blinded me with science.")

Most of the cards I threw into the blue rolling garbage can. I figure if some undocumented worker grabs the Medicare card and uses Stef's social security number to get a job, well, she'd be pleased that even in death she helped someone in worse shape. But I saved the driver's licenses and the BioGift card for a collage I have in mind. I also tossed the twelve-by-sixteen senior portrait of the son Stef gave up for adoption, a pewter-framed picture taken the day she got married for the third—or was it the fourth, I was never sure and now there's no one to ask—time (in a light blue suit on a patio in Oceanside), and a cheap, plastic-framed picture of my dead golden retriever Franklin whom Stef and Ron loved.

It's hard to know what to keep. In my office, I've got two decorative boxes jam-packed with twenty-three years of pictures from my life with my ex-wife. I rarely look at them—usually only when I'm searching for a specific picture for an essay or because of some memory that won't let me go. Really, in the eight years they've sat up on the top shelf, I've gotten them down five, possibly six times. And these are from my own life. I couldn't imagine keeping pictures from a life that wasn't mine. I suppose I could have sent them to her son or Ron's kids from an earlier marriage, but I spent most of May, June, and July divvying up the items in her house, and I'm just done with it.

Besides, in the garage is a large clear plastic tub filled with all the pictures from my own childhood. We moved this tub from Sequim to my mother's assisted living apartment and then to a storage facility after she died. My sisters asked me to look through the tub and bring some pictures for our mom's memorial. I spent about ninety minutes sifting through the years and finally couldn't take seeing another photo of the family gathered in the dining room, trying to look festive or holiday cheerful while my father glowered out from the head of the mahogany table. My sisters laughed when I relayed this—but it wasn't exactly a happy laugh. Do I send this tub back to storage? Keep it here and scan the photos? Send the photos out to a scanning service? For now, it's pushed up against the gardening supplies that I won't need until spring.

The other random box I sifted through came from my mom's assisted living apartment. The box overflowed with items I knew I'd use at some point. Laundry stain remover, Magic Erasers, Post-It notes, stamps, envelopes. That box has been sitting on the floor of the garage in front of my orange Gary Fisher mountain bike for five months, a testament to my overwhelm. At one point, I did grab the paper towels, but only to avoid walking to Safeway in the rain to buy more.

At the bottom of the box were all my clips and unpublished writing that my mom had saved. Maybe it was narcissistic of me, but all we moved from Sequim were the clips and unpublished pieces that were collected in books and journals. By the time she moved, my mom wasn't reading much and was retaining even less. On the couch cushion next to her, she stacked up two to four inches of periodicals every week. Once a month, when I'd visit her in Sequim, I'd wait until she fell asleep and then take the stack, which back then could easily grow to a foot or more high, shove it all in a brown paper grocery sack, and walk it up to the garbage can. In Portland she forgot she had a mailbox, so I'd deliver select pieces of mail each week to keep down on the clutter, which exacerbates the symptoms of Alzheimer's. All of this is to say, yes, I suppose it was narcissistic, but one way or another these clips were going to wind up in my garage.

And so I tucked the box flaps underneath each other and stuck the clips up on the shelf next to all the other clips, the Wedgewood china I've yet to bring into the house, two huge boxes of random but possibly important papers of my parents' that I have not started sorting, and a big, pre-lit wreath I bought last year for my mother's front door. As if I could orchestrate away the reality of the situation with bright lights and holiday cheer. Now, like those clips of mine and the tub of pictures, it's just another artifact in my garage.

THE WRECKAGE

Most of you reading this don't know that I played and wrote music as a kid. I traveled all over the United States, Canada, and Europe playing a handmade, pre-1978, steel-stringed Alvarez Yari (all of which means something to musicians). I understand about the circle of fifths, relative minors, and the particular delight of a well-placed B7 chord. Because of this, I like to listen to country music, which I am fairly certain everybody but Jon and the Sailor and my ex-wife will find surprising.

When I listen to country music, I hear the chords and harmonies that make my fingers itch to play. I have the great gift not of perfect pitch, but of perfect chord pitch. Play a C chord and I know it. Play in the key of A and I can tell if not from the first thrum of music, then at least by the second chord change up to E. But when I listen to country music, I also hear in the music a nostalgia for an America I'm not sure ever truly existed—even in the age of my grandparents. It is an America that is kind and is gentle, that loves lemonade and misogynistic stereotypes of women (in their cutoff shorts and their ruby red lips). It is an America that believes the flag and pickup truck will solve all our problems.

Now, I won't argue about the pickup truck (I'd also add a Carhartt jacket to the list), and I'm pretty sure driving through the high desert in a Ford F150 crew cab with heated leather seats is about the best thing out there. But this isn't about the Steens and the solace of open spaces. This is about country music. And—road trips aside—I think what makes country music so appealing to people is that it offers simple solutions to complex problems. Wrap yourself in the flag and stay safe from border-hopping Syrians, bomb-carrying

Frenchmen, and job-stealing Mexicans that Donald Trump, the Orange Jesus, keeps yelling about.

But it turns out that the Syrians, and the French, and the Mexicans love country music too. In fact, there's a *Radiolab* episode about the popularity of American country music in countries ranging from Australia to Thailand to Zimbabwe. On the show, anthropologist Aaron Fox suggests that the genre's surprising cross-border appeal is related to its universal themes of migration, regret, and longing for home.

This surprises me, sort of. I say *sort of* because if you simply listen to the music—the minor sevenths and the diminished chords playing out or, as The Judds sing, "The slide of a steel guitar . . . the moan of an old blues harp"— you understand the power of the music itself to evoke emotion. "The [pedal] steel guitar is the signature sound of country because it's recognized as iconic of a crying human voice," Fox says.

I guess if country music is less about nostalgia for Morning in America than it is about feeling grief and longing, it makes sense that I'm listening to Sirius XM's Outlaw Country, Prime Country, and The Highway so much lately. Because, well, as the Ironman says, "Dead mom. Holidays."

But it's not just that. It's the magnitude of the loss of this past year and the depth of the ensuing silence. When I had dinner with Stan Rubin last week, widower of Judith Kitchen, he asked if I was crying much. I allowed as how I cry a drop or two a day. It wasn't a euphemism. Truly, I usually only eke out a drop or two and sometimes not even that—usually I just feel the grief in my chest, but no tears will come.

Stan nodded and reminded me of a line from

Wordsworth's "Ode: Intimations of Immortality," *A silence too deep for tears*. Then he laughed, because he and Judith were anything but quiet, and he said, "Actually, the line is 'thoughts that do often lie too deep for tears.' But it may as well be silence."

Yes, it may as well. And in the place of that silence I find solace in country music. The other morning, I remembered my father used country music as solace and catharsis as well. He used to drive around in a gold Lexus sedan—the very antithesis of an F150—listening to country songs on the FM radio. One time he told me about a country song that broke his heart. "Kaydoos," he said. "It was so sad I had to pull over and break down." The double entendre of that line used to crack me up, but I also always respected that my dad—big and hulking, with hands that shook from nerves the Office of Naval Intelligence ruined him with—never hid his emotions, specifically his tears and his great sadness.

I have no idea what song wrecked my dad so badly he had to pull over and sob into a white handkerchief that I know perfectly well to be an artifact of imagination. Perhaps it was Vince Gill's "When I Call Your Name." Silence, loss, sorrow. It may as well have been.

ALL-YOU-CAN-EAT BUFFET

"Kate, you don't want to be stuck eating scraps from the table of joy." That's what my damn therapist said to me after I'd been explaining how I think what I was the most attracted to in my last girlfriend, the Tines, was that her eyes radiated joy.

The Tines has a face that has been tempered by life's struggles—a Mohs scar on her right cheek, a certain tiredness around her deep-set eyes that is more pronounced every March. You probably wouldn't even notice this, but I studied this face so closely.

All of the Tines's skirmishes with life, with living, have not seemed to diminish her capacity for joy. If anything it has deepened it because she knows death so intimately, knows how lives can change in an instant. And when she smiles, the color of her eyes electrifies, and the lines around the corners of her eyes crinkle up in the most authentic and delightful way—you know the way someone's eyes do when they are really, truly smiling, when they are authentically happy. You can't fake that.

The story that I tell myself is that I haven't felt a lot of joy these past few years. Oh, I have my moments, but it hasn't been sustained, right? And there are lots of reasons for this, lots of which you can read about, and lots of which you'll never know because even though it appears that I wear my heart on my sleeve, well, it's not all out there.

I feel like I haven't been able to tap into the consistent joy I saw in the Tines or in my golden retriever, Franklin. Each time I picked up the leash, each time I said, "Do you want to . . ." it didn't matter what the rest of that sentence was. Of course he wanted to. Whatever it was—a ride to the dry cleaner, a walk around the block, hanging out together in the garden—Franklin wanted to, was happy to. His whole body radiated joy.

Same with the Tines. And this joy—when she smiled—it filled my own heart right up in a way I hadn't really felt since probably before my dad died. That's when responsibility fell on my shoulders like nobody's business. And I forgot joy. Or joy forgot me. But really it's probably the former.

But what my therapist pointed out to me was that it had not gone away, joy I mean. There are all these moments: Reading my book to a room full of queers. Standing up to a verbally abusive woman. Riding my bike with new friends. Riding my bike with old friends. Laughing so hard with Lesbiana Profundis that I almost had to pull the car over—laughing for five more miles because we are so damn funny. Connecting with the women in the cast of *Listen to Your Mother*. My daily Facebook conversation with the Alaskan Poet. This crow that keeps landing on the tree right outside my office and looking in the window and cawing at me—every single day. A girl and a band singing "Folsom Prison Blues" in the key of E while sequestered from the bar patrons behind a cage made of chicken wire. Spontaneous dinners with old friends. This incredible dress I saw a woman wearing the other night—that tastefully showed her décolletage and a bit of her thigh each time she crossed her legs, and made me raise my eyebrows and suck in my breath just a little each time I noticed it. The loving embrace of a group of women in suits.

What my therapist meant was that joy is everywhere in my life, but it isn't sustained because that's simply not possible. She meant why are you thinking the only place to find joy is in one other person. She meant that I have a Sunday buffet of joy in my life, complete with prime rib carving station and chocolate fountain, so why would I limit myself to just one item on the menu. You can fill up at the buffet and then later, when you are a little hungry again, remember how you got three different kinds of salad, prime rib and ham, and then went back for fruit and bacon and potatoes O'Brien, and finally finished off with chocolate pudding and gluten-free graham crackers dipped in the chocolate fountain (because this is Portlandia, after all). She meant that we all have this, all the time, in our own way. So why would we want to eat scraps from the table of someone else's joy. Because we have our own table of joy, but we have to eat in moderation, in doses. It's homeopathic. That's how it's supposed to be. The trick—like everything else—is to notice it.

THE TWENTY-TON SHIELD

I fight the voice of the oppressor every day. That voice has opinions on everything. On writing. (You should craft these essays more carefully.) On eating. (Should you really eat toast when you had a metric shit-ton of watermelon? That is not the way to your goal.) On bike riding. (Your knee wouldn't hurt so much if you dropped those pounds back off, and you'd also be faster.) On how I do or don't clean the kitchen, do or don't fold the laundry, do or don't speak to my beloveds, do or don't—well, you get the point.

We are *crushed* by perfectionism in this culture. Absolutely crushed by it. I see it everywhere and in everyone (men and women)—from the random overheard conversation in Starbucks to the friend who's trying to write a blog and has rewritten a single five-hundred-word post more than seven times. ("I make it better each time," she says. *No, you don't*, I think.) We think that we must do the thing, whatever the thing is, perfectly. And if we don't, we are failures. That blog writer I told you about? She said, as if to defend her incessant editing, "I've only ever received As. I can't put something out there that isn't perfect."

But this is the voice that actually keeps us stuck, keeps me stuck. Keeps me from going to the gym because I only have thirty minutes instead of an hour. Keeps me from publishing because it isn't grade A material. Keeps me from riding my bike fifty-two miles on a Saturday morning because it will take too long since I'm slower than I used to be.

Everything colludes to keep us "perfect." Media, our puritanical American roots, the pressure we put on each other. Like most of the things I write about, I don't know the solution to the problem, except to keep calling it out, to keep honoring ourselves, honoring myself for simply trying. This morning I read about perfectionism, and one of the things the author asserted was, instead of looking at 100 percent as perfect (and, not really attainable in most matters), why not start from 0 percent and then add. What would make you 1 percent better today? On Friday, that meant my decision to go to the gym for a quick thirty-minute weight session. I almost didn't go because I didn't have *enough* time to *really* work out. But where would that have left me? Is a week of thirty-minute workouts better than a week of no workouts because I couldn't squeeze in an hour a day?

Brené Brown says about perfectionism, "It's a twenty-ton shield we lug around thinking that it will protect us when, in fact, it's the thing that's really preventing us from flight."

Stop lugging the shield. And if you see me or someone else lugging a shield, help us set it down.

ON SOFTENING

I've been thinking about gratitude lately. One of the things the Opera Singer and I did most evenings before we went to sleep was "appreciations." It's a technique from psychologist Harville Hendrix—a way, he says, that we can deepen relationships, and since that time with Opera Singer, I've used it with friends, clients, lovers. In stressful situations where I am trying to change the energy or at a birthday party where the mood is festive and the party girl is being feted. Quietly in a cool, dark bedroom with a beloved or in a conference room lit with fluorescent lights and full of engineers.

The formula is pretty simple. It goes like this: "Kate Carroll de Gutes, of the many things I appreciate about you, today I appreciate . . ." And here you list the simplest things, the things you notice and, if you are like me, so often fail to mention: that you folded the pile of laundry on the chest in the hall, that you replaced the empty toilet paper roll, that you made me a café au lait with soy milk in the big green mug that I love so much.

Something happens when we're grateful and when we're being appreciated. We soften. If you are doing the appreciation, it forces you to carefully notice the many ways another person is thoughtful. And if you are being appreciated, it makes you light up at the ways someone has seen you for who you really are.

I know this to be true for myself. When the Opera Singer would begin, before she was even through my middle name, drawing out the A the way the diction teachers at the National Theater Conservatory taught her—sounding like the linguists intended, but sounding so patrician to my ear— I would feel my entire being relax. And I have seen the beatific smile the Ironman still gets on her face—still, although we are no longer lovers—when I say to her, "ZG, of the many things I appreciate about you . . ." She grins and hisses out a little rush of breath and drops her eyes, and I know exactly how her heart is opening because I feel that same opening in myself when I am being appreciated.

And I think the root of it is kindness. We live in a world where things are harsh and factionalized. (Is that even a word? Spell-check is not flagging it, so it must be.) With social media and instant messaging and texting, we've lost nuance. We take offense instantly because we can. There's so little to appreciate or notice on the interwebs, really, and so much at which to take umbrage. (Don't even get me going on white, male, Christian exceptionalism and militias in Harney County.)

I listened to an interview with the singer Carrie Newcomer and she spoke of the importance of being kind, that it is, in many ways, the greatest of the emotions. She said, "Kindness is like the country cousin to love. It does the dishes when no one asks it to."

Newcomer went on to read her poem called "Three Gratitudes." Here's the beginning of it:

> Every night before I go to sleep
> I say out loud
> Three things that I'm grateful for,
> All the significant, insignificant
> Extraordinary, ordinary stuff of my life.
> It's a small practice and humble,
> And yet, I find I sleep better
> Holding what lightens and softens my life
> Ever so briefly at the end of the day.
> Sunlight, and blueberries,

Good dogs and wool socks,
A fine rain,
A good friend,
Fresh basil and wild phlox,
My father's good health,
My daughter's new job,
The song that always makes me cry,
Always at the same part,
No matter how many times I hear it.
Decent coffee at the airport

There's so much to be grateful for if only we look, isn't there? External and internal. The sun that shone briefly today after days of ice. The man who stopped next to me to watch and remark on a wily homeless man riding a pimped-out Schwinn bike over the snow and ice. The Thai restaurant that stayed open during the ice storm and fixed me Pad Thai and Tom Kha Gai. That I am resilient enough to notice the beauty of the rain as it falls even as I miss the brilliant blue sky above the Pedernal in northern New Mexico. That you are out there reading this and feeling your own grateful thoughts.

AMERICANO, NO ROOM

My baristas are all lovely. There's Kelly, the artist and neighborhood activist who gave me a great tip about traveling to Venice during the biennale, and Amy, who is tall and quiet and, I just learned, is a mom. There is Katy, another mom who has worked for Starbucks for seventeen years because the benefits are so good. And there is the Child Barista.

The Child Barista's mother died when the kid was only seventeen years old. Her mom was a single parent, an alcoholic who'd finally gotten sober and was, ironically, killed by a drunk driver, leaving the Child Barista unexpectedly on her own. She moved in with her boyfriend and learned quickly that her mother's social security death benefit didn't go very far. But this kid is pretty amazing. She dumped the boy—he was physically abusive—left Southern California and got herself to Oregon, where her maternal grandmother lives. She's attending Portland Community College, making coffee, and walking dogs in order to make ends meet. She's only twenty-one and the amount of stuff she's had to figure out on her own reminds me daily of my privilege.

This kid has questions. About life, writing, money, cancer, aging. I wait for my triple tall Americano and lean up against the back of the warm espresso machine while she pulls shots and steams 2%.

"Kate, can I ask you a question?" Every single time. And every time I have to stop myself from saying, "You just did."

Recently she said, "I want to go to Italy next year to celebrate my dead mom's fortieth birthday, and I need to understand how to really save money."

I love that this kid would ask me this. But did you

catch that? Her mother would be eleven years younger than I am. Then she tells me her grandma is fifty-six. Fifty-six! That's only five years older than I am. Her grandma probably entered menopause about ten minutes before I did.

But I helped get the Child Barista squared away with a savings plan, something my own parents never talked to me about. Every week she tells me how much she has earned in tips and has put into her Italy account and how she never realized that she could pay for a whole trip with just tips.

Today she told me she wanted a new job. She wants to cook at a vegan restaurant. I said, "Listen, honey, you're twenty-one. When you're thirty, you're going to want a job that isn't so hard on your body. I know you can't conceptualize this right now, but you have to trust me that your feet and back are going to be killing you in just nine years." She allowed as how even now it sucks to stand all day long.

"Maybe you're right, Kate. Maybe I don't want to work in a service job the rest of my life."

I feel grateful that I can offer this kid insight and advice, serve as a sounding board for her and give back to her some of the generosity that's been given to me over the years. Where would I be without my circle of older and wiser friends? People willing to share their own lessons without any attachment to whether I take their advice or not.

And that's the thing. Sometimes all we want is to know that someone else walked a similar path and came out the other side. My best therapist routinely says to me, "I can't offer you anything except a story about . . . ," and here you can insert my current worry, fear, obsession, or grief. This is phenomenally comforting to me. Better than any advice. (The world is full of advice on what to do. Just look at the Internet.) And one time when I was crying so hard about my mom and what to do and trying to talk it out, she looked me right in the eyes and directed all her energy at me and said, "You're doing just fine, Kate. Really." It cost me $100, but I hung onto those two sentences like a lifesaving ring—and sometimes I still pull them out and repeat them to myself.

I think about that when I tell the Child Barista to save her tips or to consider working in the Netflix call center. ("What would I do, talk to people about DVDs all day long? Like, 'Girl, you behind on your $9.99. Do you want your movies or what?'") We never know what it is people are going to hang on to, which story or bit of road map is going to change the trajectory of a life.

The Child Barista asks me questions because I look her in the eyes, instead of looking at my phone. For the three minutes it takes her to make my coffee, she tells me about her mother because I give her my full attention. It costs nothing and enriches me more than reading my email ever will.

LET US EAT CAKE

Because I live in #Portlandia, it's easy for me to get gluten-free everything. No, really. Pizza, bread, cupcakes, cookies, bagels, sauces, pie, dinner rolls, crackers, noodles, and Bundt cake. I love Bundt cake, its ridged shape, its dense texture and bite, its light use of glaze.

In the middle to late seventies, my mother used to make Bundt cakes all the time. She bought a Teflon Bundt cake pan and went to town with recipes: cinnamon swirl, Kentucky butter, lemon lift, sour cream coffee cake. All but the latter typically had a rum glaze. I never liked the taste of the rum glaze (and really, what ten-year-old likes rum?), so maybe that's why I'm always delighted when the Bundt cakes at New Cascadia don't have much glaze on them. It's the cake I'm after, with its firm, well-browned edges and moist interior.

I like these cakes, also, because they're just sweet enough, and they usually have a vanilla base, and vanilla-like desserts are my favorite. But, it wasn't until today—a sunny February day, warm enough that I could stand outside without a coat or even a light jacket—that I realized I associate these cakes with summer and with my mother being happy.

She baked a lot back then, I think. Bundt cakes, brownies with frosting made from Hershey's chocolate syrup, Bisquick shortcakes, popovers at brunch. Maybe she still thought there was hope for happiness in her marriage. (I can hear her in my head even now and it makes me want to censor myself, "We were happy, Katie. We weren't the Cleavers, but we were happy enough.") Maybe it was because she still sat in the center of a big community of friends. Maybe it was that Northern California was just sunnier back then—certainly brighter than the Pacific Northwest. I don't know, but I feel wistful and content at once imagining her back then, moving purposefully through our dark, tidy kitchen, her white vinyl flip-flops ("go-aheads" in her parlance) slapping against her heel with each step. A stack of LPs dropping one after another, blasting out Fats Domino, Eddie Rabbit, Carly Simon, Paul Simon, Ray Charles. The kitchen window open, the family room slider too, music reaching us in the backyard. We didn't have a pool in those years, but in my memory, that's where we are, floating in the green-bottomed, free-form pool or hanging onto the river rock edge of her design, talking, laughing, drinking from the only glasses that she allowed us to use poolside—clear plastic with brown and orange polka dots, a perfect complement to the table umbrella. My mother was nothing if not coordinated.

But that isn't entirely true, is it? She was depressed even back then, feeding her kids too late into the summer night. Dinner at 8:00 p.m. because it was too hot to eat earlier, a scoop of bay shrimp salad mounded on a piece of romaine lettuce. Eating by candlelight at the redwood picnic table—because why wouldn't you cut down a redwood tree to make a picnic table? This was the seventies, after all—my mom, my sisters, and me. My dad is never in these memories. Maybe because he's been dead almost six years now, maybe because it wouldn't be as relaxed if he were in the picture. It's hard to say.

Without my mother to ask, my memories and neurons are remaking the stories of Bundt cakes and summer and late dinners on hot nights. And even if my mom were here, would she remember? Would she recall that she always kept the Bundt cake pan in the cardboard box it came in? That the box had sky-blue writing on it? Would she know that we sold it in the estate sale because her children don't bake and it's hard enough to make a regular cake much less a gluten-free one? I don't know. I guess I don't have to know. I can just enjoy the tooth of blueberry lemon Bundt cake from New Cascadia Bakery on a sunny day in February.

IV.

Spring

MOTHER'S DAY

Your mother made your school lunch for you all the way through your senior year of high school, and she always drew her signature smiley face on the paper napkin she put in your lunch bag. Your mother fed and clothed you to the best of her ability (even when that "ability" meant TV dinners and sleeveless, aqua-colored dresses). Your mother made you a Halloween costume out of dryer venting, a box covered in tinfoil, and a colander, and it won the school prize for being the best (especially compared to all the store-bought Bionic Man and Bionic Woman costumes). Your mother helped you every day with your algebra homework until you finally passed the class—the fifth time you took it. Your mother did some good shit. You love your mother.

Your mom, she said you were a whiner with a low pain threshold, so she made you walk around for three days on an avulsed Achilles tendon before she finally took you to the orthopedist. Or, maybe your mom left your nine-year-old self alone all day when you had pneumonia, and then the power went out and the wind was blowing and it was dark and you were scared, so you walked in a nightgown, barefoot through the snow to the neighbor's house. Or maybe your mom told you she was going on vacation for two weeks and that your fifteen-year-old brother was in charge, then she didn't come back for two years. Your mother did some bad shit. You still love your mother.

And then your mother upped and died. And suddenly you are crying all the time, unexpectedly. At the post office. At the grocery store. At the gym (because this kind of grief is cellular, my friends). At Les Schwab (you get really fast service when this happens). At sushi. At the assisted living facility (after they've removed your mom's hospital bed and you see a tiny pair of slippers that her feet won't ever slide into again). At the sink in a stranger's kitchen (hunched down like a troll, your head resting on the cool porcelain of the deep farmhouse sink, trying to catch your breath before going on to read to a crowd of mostly unknown people). On the phone with Social Security. Talking to USAA Survivor Relations. ("First, let me say, I am sorry for your loss." *Oh god, please don't say that.*) Talking to the idiots at DIRECTV (and telling the account rep, *I will use social media to systematically destroy your organization if you don't cancel this account this fucking minute*, which automatically escalates you to a call supervisor who can usually help you better).

When the endorphins kick in on a bike ride or on a run in the desert. When it is too hot, when it is too cold, when it is raining, when it is sunny. When the tulips you smuggled back from Amsterdam begin to bloom. When you are in a clubby bar full of red leather banquettes and dapper queers and a torch singer begins with notes all sultry, "Pack up all my cares and woes, feeling sad, here I go, bye, bye, blackbird." (Which, for the record, gets the Alaskan Poet, too, who lost both her parents in one year.)

When a really, really kind woman on the other end of the phone gently mentions the way you are trying to control the world in order to stay safe, and that it is truly an impossibility, that we are all inherently unsafe, on the verge of death at any moment, and that no superpower in the world will keep this from happening. Then you cry super hard, bent in half at the waist, head resting on the end of bed, trying to gasp silently so she won't hear you (but she does—unfortunately, fortunately, it's okay, really, keep breathing, you're allowed to cry, I swear to god, she's not judging you). And she knows that untethered feeling. It might not be the exact same untethered feeling as your own—but she knows it—because even as her mom is still alive, there were years when she may as well not have been.

See, in some ways we're all figuring out how to mother ourselves.

Yes, that sounds New Age. But, it's the truth.

Who really got what she wanted from her mother? Your mother was human, is human, and is beautifully, inherently flawed because of this. That's what makes her authentic, and it's what makes your grief authentic. So go ahead and cry this Mother's Day. For your mom. For my mom. For all the moms and all the kids. And if you don't do it at the gym or the gas station or the food carts or bent in half with your head resting on the end of the bed, that's okay. Just do it. It's the least and the best you can do.

THE LOST ARTS

On my desk I have a needlepoint glasses case that was my maternal grandmother's. I can't remember when my mother gave it to me—sometime in the last nine years when I started wearing Costco reading glasses for looking at things like the dosing directions on pill bottles and the emergency numbers on the backs of credit cards. (Don't you think they should put those "Call us if your card is stolen" phone numbers in a bigger point size?)

I never remember my grandma doing crafts like this, but I know she did because I have this and a few other things she made—like a white wool felt Christmas tree skirt with hand-sewn sequined trees and sleighs, Santas and reindeers, candy canes and snowmen, along with a green velvet wall hanging with a hand-pieced and hand-sequined "Noel" running down the middle of it. It's one of the few things my sisters and I fought about. It's so elegant, and it always hung above the Baldwin spinet in my grandmother's living room and then was reprised in the exact same spot in our own living room after my grandmother died. And we all wanted it. It's an iconic image from our childhood and a symbol of the best of our family. So we agreed to share it. I didn't decorate last Christmas, grief and all that, so I didn't hang it—but I know right where it will go this year. And I can imagine where it will be in Sue's house in 2018 and in Jule's in 2019.

But this glasses case. I kind of forgot about it. It's tucked next to a cherrywood desktop organizer I have—I got it at Levenger's to hold a dictionary and thesaurus, my day calendar, and my checkbook in the upright slots. You know, in the days before pervasive Internet and thesaurus.com, Google calendar, and online bill pay. There are also two little drawers and in one are all the business cards for every position my father ever held and also every business card for every position I ever held. Again, back when they gave out business cards and people had "positions" like "Account Coordinator" and "President." (To be fair, people do still work jobs with these titles, but they don't usually get business cards—much less cards with gold embossed logos printed on gray linen paper.)

Anyway, the organizer sits at an angle on the desktop, and so there is a tiny space to the left of it and the edge of the desk, which is butted up against the wall. The needlepoint glasses case was here, standing upright and empty. And for some reason I pulled it out and took a look at it. It's a beautiful butter yellow with a needlepoint rectangular frame the color of spring peas that runs around the front edge. In the middle is a girl who appears to be holding onto stems of flowers on either side of her. The flowers arch up and over her like one of those big balloon arches that cyclists on the Tour de France ride under at the end of a stage. But because this is needlepoint, the girl and the flowers appear very pixelated, and because I am the generation I am, I cannot help but think that this girl would be at home in a 64-bit version of Super Mario Brothers or Donkey Kong. But she just sits there. She doesn't jump up and try to knock gold coins out of the flowers over her head. She's just there, a reminder of a lost art.

But here's the really weird thing. This case is lined with green felt, and it must have lived in my grandmother's purse for years. Or maybe it was in her dresser and she didn't use it, but it seems unlikely, because it smells so much like her face powder. I'm not even sure why I stuck my nose right into the opening, but I did. And there it was, a mix of Elizabeth Arden and wool and that sweet undertone of

Kleenex. And bam, I could feel my own cheek pressed against the cool, plush, soft cheek of my grandmother, smell her, call up the feeling of love and safety I felt every time I was next to her.

Maybe we can always do this, but it felt so visceral this morning because I was just with all my dear, dear friends at AWP, which is a writers' conference on steroids. Fifteen thousand writers all crammed—this year, at least, every year it is somewhere different—but crammed nevertheless into the LA Convention Center, with all the writer neuroses and comparisons and fears and publishing contracts won and lost, all in one giant space all at once. It is almost too much, but not quite. And there was so much laughing and so much crying, sometimes both at once. Because in this last year there has been death and cancer and breakups and injuries and illness and, and, and.

On Saturday night the Alaskan Poet and I had dinner with some very important poets, one of whom is our lovely and generous friend who used to have the very important title of Writer Laureate of Alaska and who had cancer this past year. These people we were dining with—in an LA restaurant serving country French food like steak au poivre and green lentil salad—were fifteen to twenty-five years older than the Alaskan Poet and I. And our friend, a Very Important Poet, really the most important poet of all because she is our friend and we love her so much, she invited us along because that's who she is—a connector, a networker. She also loves us and knows that at AWP sometimes the only chance you have to visit is to squeeze someone's hand once under the dinner table.

The Alaskan Poet and I, we sat at the end of the table. Like the kids. And we were orphans. We are orphans. Here were all these adults, and we were listening to them talk and get caught up and reminisce about how they met thirty-five years earlier, and in some ways it was like being fifteen and being invited to your parents' dinner party. You listened and sometimes you threw a word in edgewise, but mostly you shut up and gathered info.

The next morning at the airport, I saw the Very Important Poet. She was flying Southwest Airlines to Arizona and I was flying Southwest to Oregon, and I told her our dinner observation. She felt badly that we'd not interacted much, but I quickly explained that it was awesome. That for one moment, two fifty-something orphans felt like everything was right with the world because of the murmur of old friends, bread with butter, chocolate mousse, and learning about how Rita Dove once came to a house party where there was no furniture except a futon because the Very Important Poet once was not so important and was struggling to get by and all she could afford was a futon (and hearing stories like these when you are fifteen—or fifty-one—is like hearing secret adult information). And that now, thirty years later, there are poems and steak and laughing and crying and a needlepoint glasses case that can bring back my birth family and my chosen family all at once.

DON'T THINK TWICE

So in the morning you are a finalist for the Oregon Book Award and then at lunchtime you find yourself in a super chichi Portland neighborhood in a black hoodie and your Haflinger slippers—or your boiled wool clogs, as some of you might like to call them. And then you realize that you have to increase the size of your Word document to 150 percent so that your aging eyes can see the letters and words as they march across the screen. And then you realize that you are coming down with the mother of all colds and you have to go lie down.

All of this is to say, after the ecstasy, the laundry. (Actually, Jack Kornfield said that.) No one's life changes simply because they have been nominated for a prize and are standing on the shoulders of giants.

When I was a young writer who wasted all the time in the world *not* writing in coffee shops, I used to imagine how this day would feel. I was right about the feeling—thrilling and unreal—but wrong about the lasting effects. This morning I'm still thrilled and a bit befuddled. I'm also still just as worried that my work is derivative and trite and meaningless. I'm sad that my parents are dead and don't get to celebrate this with me, *and* I'm grateful that my dead parents don't get to celebrate this with me. Because try explaining "writing lens" and how "imposing a narrative necessarily changes a memory and the subsequent story" to the people you are writing about.

And really, it doesn't matter what I write. Some people are upset I've written about them. Others are upset that I haven't written about them (and wonder when I will). Still others are upset that I've written something they thought was about them when, in fact, they were the farthest thing from my mind. What I'm saying is, you just have to do the work and not think about the people you are writing—or not writing—about. You must do the work and not think about the Oregon Book Award or the Lambda Literary Award or the Next Generation Indie Publishing Award. Because, it's about the work. Literally. It is about stringing words together on the page.

Today I talked with my other therapist. Yes, I have two. One who is narrative driven and a practicing Jungian—myths, storytelling, and all that—and one who has a whole host of therapeutic tools to help rewire, quite literally, your neural network. This man, my second therapist, is both Jewish and Buddhist (just think of him as JB for short). Really, JB is the most placid individual I've ever met. It's like all the ancestral drama and trauma of the Jews has been replaced by the Buddhist lineage part, and JB just sits there calmly in his black leather chair with a most inscrutable look on his face and listens to whatever I relate. Today he was asking me how I felt about being a finalist for the Oregon Book Award, and I said, "Honestly, I felt like a poseur because writing the book wasn't that hard." Now, mind you, I just finished the hardest year of my life—two estates and three eulogies later, a book seems like a simple task.

JB said to me, "Kate, I actually got kind of excited for you, that you said it was easy. Because it's what you're meant to do. And so what if you don't agonize over every single sentence like Anthony Doerr, erasing and erasing, chasing perfection." (Well, okay, I inserted Anthony Doerr here. He didn't really reference Doerr, but I had just attended a Doerr lecture where he let us in on his editing process, and let me say that's why *All the Light We Cannot See* won the Pulitzer, and I merely write these essays. Because Doerr, he is a master craftsman who agonizes over every single word. Anyways, I digress, and besides JB said everything except the phrase "like Anthony Doerr.")

JB continued. He said, "Kate, I think what resonates with people is your rawness. It's like Dylan. He recorded stuff in a single take and changed the words on the fly. One time, in an interview, Emmylou Harris said she was humming the backup because Dylan changed the song on the fly, and she didn't know the words. Do you think Dylan thinks he's a poseur?"

I allowed as how this was one of those trick therapy questions. Because the only reasonable answer is "No, Dylan thinks he's Dylan." But still, I tried to weasel my way out. "Well, you know, every artist has paralyzing self-doubt," I said. I dropped my chin and looked up and out at him in sort of a beseeching isn't-my-self-doubt-charming sort of way.

Then, I came home and Googled "Dylan on self-doubt." You know, to bolster the argument that I was now having in my head with JB. I found an article written by Brett Duncan that said,

> Bob Dylan is a legend. You could argue that he is easily one of the five most influential musicians ever. And there's no arguing he's one of the most prolific songwriters who's ever lived. Bob Dylan changed music. . . . But here's the revolutionary part. Bob Dylan is ugly as sin. He literally looks like a rat. His voice is absolutely horrible. Seriously, have you ever heard anyone hear Bob Dylan sing and respond with, "Oh, that's the most beautiful sound I've ever heard?" Most of us can't even understand what he's saying. We need an interpreter. He's polarizing (people love him or hate him). He ignores trends. . . [But], Bob Dylan produced. He put it out there. He

didn't wait for perfection. He knew what he had did no good sitting on the dock. He kicked it out the door and gave it a shot at success.

So, I'm trying to own it: Once I sat down and did it, the book wasn't that hard to write. And people like it. And I put it out there without waiting for perfection. I kicked it out the door and gave it a shot at success. Even though it's wearing a black hoodie and Haflinger slippers. Even though its parents are dead. Even though, even though.

MUCH, MUCH LESS

Who knows what enlightenment is? I used to think that "enlightened" people were those who maintained equanimity in the shit-storm of life. You know, when you've accidentally caught on fire the towel you're using in lieu of a hot pad (because you left all those behind when you got divorced, not thinking about hot pads, just thinking about the trauma of ending), and Pandora is playing some terrible Sara Bareilles song that is breaking your heart, and your neighbor is smoking a cigarette and the smoke is shooting straight through your open balcony door, and you miss your ex-girlfriend so much that you're crying a little, but you're also trying to put out the actual fire and you burned up a towel that your ex-ex-ex-girlfriend's mother gave you for Christmas, and oh, yeah, you just stepped on the tiny foot of your dead mother's cat (who is dying herself). In this situation, an enlightened person would just breathe and repeat some mantra about being able to find a point of balance in any situation, and then maybe use the flames from the towel to light a candle on her altar.

Or, maybe, enlightenment looks like a person who sees the best in everyone, even the sullen checker at Safeway who never says hello and always stares at you like you are the enemy because you are buying million-dollar organic chicken and gluten-free waffles. Or maybe enlightenment looks like a woman who never gets upset and flips off the truck driver who pushes his way into her lane on the St. John's bridge climb; or maybe it looks like someone who never wishes that the woman who sent her a nasty email would maybe, just maybe, trip and smash her elbow really hard on the doorjamb into her office where she pretends to be the adjudicator of mental health.

But I think what I realized on my bike ride yesterday afternoon—it was fifty-six degrees and sunny and all the flowering cherry trees are blooming in their brilliant pinks and whites—is that for me enlightenment is perhaps just noticing these things. Noticing the impulse to flip off the car that drives too closely to you and forces you to ride in gravel—and then breathing through it. Noticing the impulse to want to call the ex-girlfriend because you miss her so goddamned much, but knowing it still isn't time—and breathing through it. Noticing your head exploding because you still haven't fixed that one paragraph in the essay that is now two weeks late—and breathing through it. Noticing how much you miss your dead mom who never really truly knew who you were but still missing her so much—and breathing through it. Noticing how totally good a gluten-free stroopwafel would taste, salivating really, but knowing you need to fit into your suit for the Oregon Book Awards—and breathing through it. Enlightenment, I think, is realizing that thoughts are just thoughts, and you don't have to do anything but notice, name, and let go.

When the Opera Singer left me so unceremoniously, I tried meditation to calm the hamster wheel in my head that said I was dying, that I was worthless, that I was a bad butch. But all it did was ratchet up my anxiety because, by trying to get quiet, the thoughts came at hyper speed. Then JB introduced me to Adyashanti. Adyashanti doesn't think that it is possible to stop your thoughts or that enlightenment looks like we think it does.

Here's what he said about enlightenment at a lecture he gave in Portland: "Freedom is not necessarily exciting; it's just free. Very peaceful and quiet, so very quiet. Of course, it is also filled with joy and wonder, but it is not what you imagine. It is much, much less."

THE POWER OF SECRET WEAPONS
AND OTHER THINGS YOU DIDN'T LEARN
IN SCHOOL

I got to go to an honest-to-god cocktail party, hot hors d'oeuvres and all, for the Oregon Book Award Finalists. Of course, getting a group of introverts in a room and trying to make them mix is like trying to teach a pig to sing. (It wastes your time and, in this case, terrifies the pig.) But I was in luck because my date was also my secret networking weapon.

So when I walked in the room and saw Brian Doyle—Brian I-gave-the-keynote-address-at-NonFiction-Now-and-how-did-this-no-name-butch-writer-get-up-for-the-same-creative-nonfiction-award-as-I-did Doyle—I said, "Oh, my god, there's Brian Doyle!" and tried to go into the other room to hide. But my Secret Weapon blocked my passage and said, "Go over there right now and introduce yourself!" I allowed as how I would do that and then at the last minute tried to twist away and said, "I can't, I can't, oh my god my legs are painted on, and I can't walk over there, and besides, there's not enough air in this room."

But the Secret Weapon has her own secret. She's socially anxious too. Only, she just puts it aside and works the room. She gave me the eye, and I said, rather morosely, "Fine. But it's not fair that I'm doing this without alcohol." And it wasn't. It isn't. Judith Kitchen used to say that the only way introverts could act like extroverts at literary conferences was with the help of alcohol. But even that only helped so far because then there was all the ex post facto shakiness with the hangovers, the guilt, and the worry about disinhibition.

At the cocktail party I was extra lucky, getting all the

shakiness and worry without any alcohol. I had to introduce myself to Brian Doyle with only a glass of still water for courage. Uncertain, feeling conspicuous in a bright red tie, I walked up and all these words rushed out at once. "Hey, I'm Kate Carroll de Gutes, and I loved your keynote at NonFiction Now, and maybe you remember we met at Mississippi Studios years ago when Jay Bates did *River and Sound Review* and I played a weird Russian character, and we're both finalists in the same category."

Now Brian Doyle is really the nicest, funniest man in the world—exceedingly kind and compassionate, Irish Catholic, with eyes that shine with amusement. Read his book, *Mink River*. Or read the one that will likely beat out mine for the Oregon Book Award, *Children and Other Wild Animals*. You'll be stunned at the lyricism and humor, how he can have you laughing and crying in the same sentence. So, after I sort of vomited my introduction all over his brown leather bomber jacket and shook his hand, he laughed and said in his staccato vocal way, "We're up for the same award? I hate you."

His blue eyes twinkled, and if I'd been in my right mind in that moment, I would have realized that the guy was wearing a heavy quilt-lined jacket in a room that was about eighty-five degrees because it was packed with sweating, nervous writers and their companions, and he was standing in the corner farthest from the door and the microphone (and closest to the bar)—which meant he was nervous too. But I was more nervous, so after he said he hated me and laughed and I laughed, I just sort of stared at him—because he's Brian Doyle and he gave the keynote address at Nonfiction Now (which basically means he's a Columbia River sturgeon in a backyard koi pond). Then I didn't know what else to say, so I sort of just eased back into the crowd.

Later I wound up talking to William Deresiewicz, a guy who looked more nervous than any of the rest of us. He was sitting in the corner opposite of Brian Doyle, all alone, staring at his glass of wine. So I threw him a line because that's exactly what my Secret Weapon was doing for me (and besides, while she was working the room for me, too, I felt like I should do my part). Bill is a disenchanted academic who taught English at Yale and Columbia—very smart, very droll. Just the kind of guy I love talking with. It was easy to chat, and we talked about being finalists, and then he said, "Is this your first book?" I told him it was the first to be published and that I had painful stories about the other two that I could tell him if he wanted to come with me to my therapist's office.

He asked how many years I'd been writing. "You mean how long did it take to get this manuscript done?" I said.

"No, no. How many years have you been writing?"

I said that this year, 2016, was the thirtieth year of me writing in earnest, for publications of one sort or another.

"Thirty years? You've been writing thirty years and this is your first book?" At this point, I kind of wished the guy would give me a swig from his glass of red wine. "That's totally amazing," he said. "You are amazing."

This wasn't the answer I expected.

He said, "Most people would just give up if they couldn't get a book published. Maybe they'd write for ten years, but they certainly wouldn't write for thirty. You have fantastic determination."

I didn't want to burst his bubble and say that part of the reason that I didn't have a published book before now was because when the others got rejected, I did sort of give up, and just went back to writing little pieces like this, publishing them in obscure journals that would never land me a book contract. I didn't want to tell him there were a few years when I didn't write a single essay, when I only penned into my journal depressing missives about the state of my marriage, my parents' illnesses, my unhappiness at my own physical health.

I didn't want to tell him all this because I thought maybe I should take what he said to heart. Maybe, even though I just turned fifty-one, it was amazing that I had been working at this for thirty years. I mean, talk about focus. But almost immediately, the death voices crept in, weaving their way into my psyche like fog rolling over the west hills. The voices that hiss about passive sentence construction and too much use of the verb "to be" and telescoping the ending and burying the lead, and if you've really been writing for thirty years, shouldn't you be better?

All of this, of course, in the span of five seconds, all of this because of a compliment (which maybe I should call a *complex-iment*—that's a little Jungian joke, in case you missed it). Probably I would have forgotten all about this interchange, but over dinner later that evening, I told my Secret Weapon, and she immediately decreed I write a post about it.

So I've been thinking a lot about it—the determination it takes to finish a book or train for a big ride or attend graduate school in your forties or close two estates in a year. And what I think is that it never occurred to me *not* to do these things, not to at least try. And that is amazing. I am saying it right here on the page. It is amazing all the things I've tried and the way I've stuck with several of them.

But, of course, that's not what all of my brain says. That nasty perfectionistic part of my brain says, *Why did it take until you were fifty to finally publish a book* and *You only rode a metric century* and *Your marriage failed because of graduate school* and *Your mom's estate wasn't very hard to close.*

And I have to stop myself right there. When I am upset I didn't publish at twenty-five, I miss feeling amazed seeing the cover of my book flashed on the big screen. When I focus on lack, I fail to see what is. And so, I'm celebrating determination, and happiness, and letting go of perfection. At least for tonight.

BEHIND THE CURTAIN

I woke up a mess today.

The book awards are going to occur in just a few days, and I read at Literary Arts with a bunch of finalists. I tried to make connections with them, to chat, to work the room like my Secret Weapon would want me to—and I did. It helped that I wasn't alone. An amazing group of queers met me for dinner and showed up at my reading: butches in bow ties and femmes in beautiful dresses (a delicious, off-the-shoulder vintage, one of them). These people I barely know came because they're awesome community builders. They came because I asked. And there we all were, queers together, plus a couple of young queer writers who used to come to my open mic, GenderFuck, and two of my baristas from the Starbucks across the street from my house. I mean, really, how lucky am I?

And yet, I felt so exposed and alone—the book, the content, my bowtie, the deaths that are written in the lines on my face and the color of my hair. And I felt so gay. I haven't felt conspicuously gay in a long time, despite the fact that I am conspicuously gay (you know, in case you haven't noticed). There is no mistaking me and my sexual orientation or my gender identity. One of the other nonfiction writers— a six-foot-tall cultural anthropologist—smiled and said, totally innocuously, "Hi, Kate." And I thought, *Oh my god, I shouldn't have worn a tie. I shouldn't be here like this. Oh my god, she is judging me so harshly. She is turning her anthropology lens on my gayness and my concept of being a boi, she is making me a study in gender.* All of this insane story inside my head while I stood there chatting with her, smiling, looking for the nearest exit.

And then there I was at the podium, under the spotlight, introducing myself, saying I don't know what. As part of a yearlong fellowship I received, I learned to practice my introductions—to give the audience a chance to get used to the sound of my voice, my cadence, and also to understand my writerly position—and how to score my work so that I could read it while sort of looking at the audience at the same time. Oh, and I learned to always practice my readings. No matter how many times you've done a piece, you should always practice. Except I didn't practice this time. So there I was, like T. S. Eliot's Prufrock, "pinned and wriggling," grasping about in the split second of synapses, then defaulting to my standard intro. And I swear to you, the people there just stared when I said my spiel about coming out in 1978 before *Will & Grace*, and Ellen DeGeneres, and before it was okay to stand up at a podium and read about ties and tuxes and all that.

I swear.

Of course, I could have had the teensiest bit of perceptual narrowing and was perhaps feeling out the room wrong, but who knows? Because, rather unusually, I read with my head mostly down, rather than looking out at the room full of literary denizens (including two other nonfiction finalists and a poet who used to be a genetic scientist!). I read about my pickup truck and hiking across the Columbia Plateau and my black Carhartt gasoline jacket and my divorce and a hat my wife knitted for me in the winter of 2004 when two feet of snow fell and then freezing rain coated everything with a thick layer of ice and we couldn't leave the house for a week.

That's what it felt like up there under the spotlight too—like I was reading up there for a week, and not the six minutes that this essay actually took to read. Up there all gay, too gay, too exposed. Whose fucking idea was this book, really? I never wanted to publish it.

No, really.

I spent five years trying to explain why it should just serve as my master's thesis and not anything else. But pieces kept getting published and Judith kept being persistent about wanting the book for Ovenbird Books. And then the writer/actress whose work I so admire insisted that the manuscript had value. And so did the editor at *Fourth Genre*. And the curator at the Jack Straw Foundation, which provided the yearlong fellowship that supposedly taught me how to better read my own work aloud. I kept getting all this validation for doing what basically feels like standing naked in public.

But fiction writers and poets tell me they feel this way, too. That readers assume all stories and poems are true because we are conditioned now by—well, don't get me started on the whole reality TV rant. My other writer friends assure me that by the time a book comes out, they hate the sound of it, are sure no one will like it or buy it, and, if they are nonfiction writers, doubt the veracity of the story told, worrying that they did not interrogate their own memories enough. Basically, that my feeling of being exposed makes sense—especially because random strangers now think they "know" me because they have read a curated version of my life.

Thank god for the Alaskan Poet. Because when I messaged her at 8:30 the next morning, she said, "It's so hard to be authentic and open. But the book is beautiful and so are you. Lots of things are going on in your life right now. Huge things. Mourning. The book. All of this light shining on it and you. And grief." Then she told me to get on my bike. So I did. I flipped my day—writing a case study in the evening—so that I could ride for three hours and look at the river and listen to the red-winged blackbirds and mourning doves and watch the osprey build their nests along the river channel markers.

I knew I needed a big cry, but the tears just wouldn't come. Instead, the grief rose and fell in my chest like waves of nausea. I stopped multiple times to look at the river and the four mountains that were out, but still I didn't cry. Then I came home and my cat crawled on my chest and my longtime oldest Portland friend, Carol, called me—Carol, whose father died of Alzheimer's; Carol who befriended my mother and visited her frequently even though my mother's apartment reeked of urine; Carol who has walked with me through death, divorce, and illness. I tried to act all casual. But she said, "What do I hear in your voice?" And that did it. I wailed. I spilled everything out to her. And my beloved friend listened and just kept saying, "Oh, honey. Oh, honey," and "Of course you feel that way," and "That makes sense," and all the right things to say to bring me back to myself until I was finally laughing.

Then I listened to some music and these lyrics to Deb Talan's song, "Big Strong Girl" caught me:

> It's not now or never
> it's not black & it's not white
> anything worth anything
> takes more than a few days
> & a long, long night
>
> don't push so hard against the world
> you can't do it all alone
> & if you could, would you really want to?
> even though you're a big strong girl,
> come on, come on, lay it down

And so to Grey and Skye, Virginia, Joe, Kristy and Lara, Jean, Kaitlyn and Adina, Kelly and Tina, Lidia, Nikole, Laura, Erin, and Carol, thank you for making the space for me to lay it down.

TRYING TO FIND HOME AGAIN

I think that I am in love with Anne Lamott, not because she is such a good writer who captures everyday moments and neuroses (she is and she does), but because she perfectly describes the landscape in which I grew up. Lamott, like no one else I have ever read, is able to write the sharp, pungent, turpentine-y scent of eucalyptus mixed with the damp briny smell of fog on a gray day. The sweet, hot smell of dried hills in mid-July. The way the sand at Stinson Beach feels soft and cold and hard all at once as the waves roll away from the shore. The magic of the Pacific (anything but) roaring in your ears as you sit on the sand at Stinson and look across to San Francisco—all magic and beckoning from this vantage—and the Golden Gate, and Sutro Tower, and the dark-treed cliffs of the Presidio.

Everything over there calling to you, the thrum of life—of lives—being played out across the water mixed with the beautiful calming waves coming and going, in and out, like your own breath, the very heartbeat of the world; the whine of gulls, the fine texture of the sand working its way under the edge of your shorts, up toward the elastic of your underwear. And Mount Tamalpais standing sentinel over all this in Marin County, seemingly never changing—visible from Highway 37 as you cut across San Pablo Bay, seen from US 101 as you speed south toward the city or north toward Novato, at your back as you sit at Stinson or Bolinas.

Lamott knows this landscape like she knows her own mind. Old Marin. The Marin I grew up in—the Marin where kids played alone all day in August-dry creek beds and caught tadpoles in the same creeks running icy in early spring. The Marin of old houses built with real two-by-fours and five-panel doors. The Marin of mourning doves and goats that need milking and chickens who roost, and, surprisingly, last night, a sight I've not seen in my hometown in years—a three-point buck with fresh velvet on his spring antlers—ambling across the road from one patch of greenbelt to another.

That's the problem: a sight I haven't seen in years.

The Marin I remember, the home to which I long to return, doesn't exactly exist anymore. My parents moved away sixteen years ago, and I felt then, feel now, like I lost the magic of Northern California—nowhere to stay, to call home, my friends all grown up, and most with families of their own now. The ranches and farms all subdivided and turned into McMansions, and the houses I imagined myself in—with redwood floors and trim ("We'll never run out of trees to log, they're huge!")—even the tiniest two-bedroom house costs $750,000 and the ones with decks shaded by oaks not killed off by the gall are well over $1 million.

And then there is the little problem of driving anywhere. And you have to drive because this is California, and Marin is a huge county outside of a proper metropolitan area, and rapid transit and bike lanes don't really exist. This means things aren't really as peaceful as they are in the story I tell myself. That's the problem with all this: it's a California that exists in my memory. It's a California that Lamott and I remember but is only recognizable in glimpses now.

And my California and Lamott's California are unrecognizable to Joan Didion, who grew up in the Sacramento delta in the forties and fifties, and who says in her essay "On Going Home," "We are talking in code about the things we like best, the yellow fields and the cottonwoods and the rivers rising and falling and the mountain roads closing when the heavy snow comes in."

But none of this is there anymore: the yellow fields

tilled up for almond groves, the cottonwoods no longer needed as wind breaks in the valley because subdivisions set at angles to each other work better than the trees ever did, I-80 and Highway 50 plowed continuously so that skiers can reach Kirkwood and Northstar and Incline.

Still, there are moments. The buck. The mourning doves. Climbing out of Terra Linda and into Novato at 11:00 p.m. with the windows of the rental car rolled down, Gillian Welch harmonizing quietly, the air warm, and that moment when you hear all the spring frogs on the dark hill right before Hamilton Air Force Base even though you are driving seventy miles per hour. It makes you feel like you are home, if only for a moment.

DEAR JUDITH

You knew all along, didn't you? And I can hear your response so quickly in my head, "Well," the *ells* drawn out all croaky and with a hint of delight at the edge of your tone. "I didn't know." (Emphasizing the empirical *know*, scientist's daughter to the end.) "But I suspected." (Rising inflection on *pected* ending in a laugh.)

Yes, Judith, you suspected that the book was good. Is good, I guess. Could possibly, might maybe win the Oregon Book Award. You imagined all those brand names, all those *objects* would resonate on a variety of levels with a wide range of readers. Straight men who tell me they'll never look the same way at the privilege of wearing a tie. Androgynous lesbians of a certain age who have been unable to find the words to express how it has felt trying to figure out how to dress all these years. Young butches—or, rather, butches who look younger than I do—showing up to my readings in ties and hats, dapper as the dapperest of queers.

You kept insisting the book had value. Every time I didn't want to publish, you raised your voice—you know, more than usual. But you didn't push, not exactly. You waited. You wanted me to come to it on my own. Until that morning in February 2014, after we'd read together the day before at the Rainier Writing Workshop's tenth-anniversary celebration. I realize now how lucky I was to share the stage with you, reading with Judith Kitchen.

I think I didn't understand because you were my friend first, not the larger-than-life literary figure that so many others saw. You were the friend who loved spies and gossip and Diet Coke and tried to make gluten-free chicken noodle soup for me when I was sick and alone in Port Townsend. The friend who tried to tell me that you understood my suffering over leaving my marriage (as you'd left yours) and how it is a uniquely painful proposition. That being left is hard. Leaving is harder. Or, if not harder, differently painful because it leaves you open to criticism and judgment.

But that morning after the reading: sitting in the lobby of the Silver Cloud Inn in Tacoma, the day brilliant, Puget Sound lapping at two sides of the hotel, the two of us at a table eating protein and veggies, drinking coffee that I'd run to Starbucks and picked up. There were three of us, though, weren't there? Stan, uncharacteristically quiet because he knew you were going for the close. Before, you'd always said, "There's always a space for you at Ovenbird." I agreed as how I knew that. But I wasn't publishing the book. This morning you said, "Look, let's do this book together. What do you think? Ovenbird. Let's do this, Kate."

I'll be honest. It's the first time it felt like a real offer. Before, I felt like you were saying publish with Ovenbird because Graywolf and Arktoi had rejected me and your agent—who you attempted to introduce me to—had actually died, and I'd failed to send the manuscript to Coffeehouse Press. This time, it felt like you really wanted the manuscript. And you knew—we both knew—the clock was winding down. At least that's the story I tell myself now. Knew it because you said, "Now, realistically, how soon can you get me revisions?" I was moving my mom the following month. I had just started a new relationship. The question: "realistically." That February morning July seemed a long way off—although less than five months. I'd already chewed and chewed on the edits. I understood, I thought, what needed to get tossed and what needed to get written. And Jesus, we both knew how well I wrote under pressure. So July.

I missed that deadline. I hadn't even finished cleaning out my mom's house by then. We renegotiated for October. Sometime in August or early September you called me. You said, "Don't miss your deadline." It scared me. I knew what it meant. I promised Halloween. I made the deadline.

ℭ

Judith Kitchen died November 6, 2014, just two days after finishing the edit on *Objects In Mirror Are Closer Than They Appear*. In her notes to me, she told me what was still missing and what to change. I followed her instructions, and it was the only time in the last nine years that I wrote and published something she didn't read for me. But her voice stayed clear in my head. I knew what to do.

Here is one of the seminal paragraphs from her final book, *The Circus Train*, published in 2013:

> You out there—I hope you're there, because I need you. I need someone to carry this project forward, to write back into a past that is beginning here. And now. You won't be using decoder rings or Our Miss Brooks on the radio. No, you'll start with smart phones and Kindles, Darth Vader movies, sneakers with lights in their heels. Digitized, somethingized—whatever will be the next science fiction in the making. Whoever you are, I hope you are watching the world go past. Your world, and your inner world within it. Look up. Take out your Bluetooth and listen. The water makes a sound as the ferry moves through it. Rips open. Overhead the mayhem of gulls is persistent. Everything persists, even as

everything changes. So keep a close watch. I'll want an accounting. I'll want to know whether memory itself can be eroded if there's no one to decode its messages, no one to sort out its meanings and give it its newly coined nouns.

I'm here, Judith. Stan is here. Matthew and William are here, and Robin and Amanda too. And Simon, Ian, and Benjamin are here in the raucous way of boys becoming teenagers becoming men. We miss you. And even though you'd hate it, we believe you're watching and are pleased with it all—the memory and the accounting, and with what persists.

V.

Summer

LOOK OVER HERE

Some of the truest words I've ever come across were written by Mary Oliver, "Doesn't everything die at last and too soon?" Everything. People, pets, plants, relationships. Everything dies. Or changes, which is like a death.

In the last nine years I've had a lot of death: my twenty-four-year marriage. My father. My relationship with the Opera Singer. My three dogs. My mentor and editor, Judith Kitchen. My friend Stef. And my mother. It's been almost eight months since she died, since I last heard her voice.

In some ways, death is easier than what I've done with my last two relationships: the slow Band-Aid-peel transition to friendship. The first was easier than the second. This one has felt like it's killing me. Partly, it's my fault. I've been unable to let her go—sort of like hanging onto the edge of the pool when you're tired and not sure you can do another lap (even when the depth is only three feet nine inches). I believed I couldn't handle more loss. I thought I couldn't get through all this grieving without being able to turn to this woman.

In some very formative ways, not starting to date until I was forty-eight has put me very far behind. It's been a hard lesson learning that you can really like someone, love them even, and find that they're still not right for you. And that breaking up and feeling okay takes constant redirection of your attention. My psyche is like a four-year-old picking at the edge of the scab, poking it constantly to see if the skin still hurts, to see if the edges have approximated, and, if they have not, what might happen if I stick a finger into the middle of it all—the finger of *if only* or *what if* or *maybe*.

Sometime during my senior year of college, I went to see a therapist at the university counseling center. My heart hid behind a wall of bravado and anger, even as I wore my feelings on my flushing cheeks and heavy frame. This woman, Peg, could see clearly the way I made myself unhappy circling 'round and 'round my personal prayer wheel of injustices and hurts. She could see that I had no idea what to do with these emotions. Except that she didn't say any of this to me. Instead, she handed me a book on meditation and suggested I read it "before you have a heart attack."

Really, who says this to a twenty-one-year-old and expects them to understand the subtext, the metaphorical value of the message? And what normal twenty-one-year-old who can finally legally buy the liquor she's been consuming since age fourteen would take a book on meditation to heart rather than a gin and tonic on the deck of a house in University Place? Which is why, at almost fifty-one, I am still a beginner at redirecting my brain, *Nope, we're not gonna think about that, look over here. Hey, I said let's go look out the window, let's think of something else until the nervous has gone out of you.* I must continually remind myself of all the joy: the sun today, the Sunday *New York Times*, the NPR Sunday Puzzle, my Soda Stream on-demand seltzer. And did I mention the sun?

I know it sounds like I am heartbroken—and I am for all sorts of reasons—but really, I am also so happy for all the reasons listed above, and for riding my bike in the sun, and for Mary Oliver reminding me that it takes vigilance and exquisite attention to combat loss. Here, look over here, and think of something else until the nervous has gone out of you.

MY FATHER WAS A DANDY

Not gay, but a man who understood the power of custom-made suits and shirts. One of my great memories is going with him to a hotel room at the Holiday Inn, San Francisco, right on the edge of Chinatown. Twice a year, a Hong Kong tailor that my dad called the "China Man" came to San Francisco, and my father would visit the tailor's hotel room, curtains closed against—against I don't know what. The sun? Other guests? The phenomenal view out toward the bay? The tailor would take my father's measurements: neck, waist, chest growing each year. This was like 1976 and in San Francisco with its huge melting pot of Chinese cultures—Mandarin, Cantonese, Hong Kongese, and Mongolian—a phrase like the "China Man" didn't raise an eyebrow, at least among the Waspy elite who were having their clothes made off-shore. These were wealthy white bankers and venture capitalists and entrepreneurs who didn't think twice about their privilege, indeed, didn't even realize that something was out of order in the world.

Spread out on a table were fabric samples: pin-striped wool in gray, blue, black, and brown; silky and light gabardines for summer weights; heavy camel hair for overcoats in tan, black, deep navy. The tailor would flip through the samples like a reader looking for a favorite passage. "I've got something you like here," he'd say in his clipped accent. And then my dad would order his suits and shirts with French cuffs, that would arrive *exactly* six weeks later, *exactly* perfect.

As I remember it, he found the tailor from a display advertisement in either the *San Francisco Chronicle* or the *Wall Street Journal*. In fact, even today, Hong Kong tailors still advertise in the *Journal*. There were lots and lots of ads, so I don't really know how my dad decided on his particular tailor, but my father stuck with this guy until his own business took off and he had enough money to have suits made by Tobias Tailors, est. 1889, 32 Savile Row, London.

I used to pore over those ads and imagine the suits I was going to have made for myself. Blue pinstripe, for sure. Something in a dark brown to match my eyes. And a tuxedo, absolutely a tuxedo. But damn, those suits were expensive, and I had this little problem: I thought you could either be butch or you could be fat, but you couldn't be both, so I shouldn't spend the money on a suit. Because even though I am butch, I am socialized as a woman in this culture and I must continually fight my own internalized shame as to how society views me and my lack of conformity to Madison Avenue's ideal. (Oh yeah, and as a rule, those Hong Kong tailors have their own discrimination going on and have routinely refused to make suits for women. Really.)

Naomi Wolf says, "A culture fixated on female thinness is not an obsession about female beauty, but an obsession about female obedience." And a big woman in a suit is failing to toe multiple lines—gender, sexual orientation, size, societal norms. So no suit for me. Until the day Saint Harridan opened a pop-up shop in Portland, and I decided I wasn't waiting any longer for a suit. I decided I didn't care if I didn't have the perfect butch body. I wanted clothes that I felt powerful in.

So I ordered a suit. It needed tailoring because the hem on the pants and sleeves on the jacket come unfinished. I found Thu Fashion, a shop run by an amazing Vietnamese woman who studied fashion in Milan and has no qualms about tailoring clothes for the LGBT community. She also has no qualms about telling you to eat a few more vegetables and hit the gym a few more times so that your "ass doesn't push on this fabric so much." Really. That's what she said. Then she threw her head back and laughed in that way that sounds almost fake, but isn't, and makes me laugh in return every time, rather than burning with shame that I am not thinner.

Today I was back in Thu's shop (her name is pronounced *Too*) with my father's tuxedos from Savile Row. One white, one black. Thu is reconstructing them so I can wear them to the Lambda Literary Awards.

Thu stood next to me, looking at me in the mirror as she pinned up the shoulders, pulled in the waist, and futzed with the jacket length. I looked at her looking at me, and we both took a breath. She patted my arm and said, "You got a girlfriend?" She saw my bottom lip start to quiver. She said, "You will when you wear this. Don't worry. Those girls are gonna go crazy when they see you in this. Listen," she said, leaning in (which isn't necessarily a good thing because Thu shouts everything—even when she's pretending to confide conspiratorially in you), "I'm gonna tell you what kind of shirt to buy and what kind of tie. You are gonna kill it. Kill it! Oh, you are gonna look so good, Cake." That's what she calls me. Cake. Which is ironic seeing I'm working out so hard to fit into these clothes.

I can't explain to you what it's like to have a straight Vietnamese woman who is dressed to the nines and sold clothes of her own design in Milan—the center of Italian fashion—pat you on the arm of your dad's tuxedo that you are having remade and act like there is nothing in the world weird about that. About a woman in a tuxedo. A woman having two tuxedos, essentially, made for her. A woman in a tuxedo who wants to look good for the ladies and the straight woman who is going to help her make it happen.

The last thing Thu shouted to me as I walked out

PERSEVERANCE

In 2012 the gym quite literally saved my life. Not for the reasons you think—the cardio, the weights, the fat loss—but because it gave me a structure, taught me about my own competitive nature, taught me about my body (and how hard I could push it and what it needed for recovery, which was, surprisingly, not always a nap but rather a slow walk to the river). But the other thing about the gym—my gym, Westcoast Fitness—was that it gave me a social structure. It gave me Jim, Jerry, Janet, and Robin in the weight room. It gave me Jan, Val, Caery, Chris, and Vee in the spin room. It gave me a nodding relationship to the other butches who were benching way more weight than I was at the time.

Every morning at 7:00, I was there either doing a strength workout or a high intensity interval workout on the bike. When I was in Sequim taking care of my mother, I worked out at the gym there. My friend Lesbro called it my religion. And maybe it was. I was paying ninety-nine dollars a month for a program called Lean Eating that gave me lessons and workouts, and when I'm paying for something, I take it more seriously.

I lost 32.5 pounds that year and more than 32 inches of girth. And then I gained it all back. You can listen to the *Risk Show* podcast and hear my story about it, "The Unbearable Lightness of Being." But I've come to realize how that essay isn't the entire story. Part of the reason I gained back my weight was that I never put myself first. I never said what I wanted or what I needed. (As an aside, the Country Music Playing Femme says that *wants* and *needs* aren't the same thing. And, semantically, I can see that she is correct, even as I struggle with this concept. So maybe the truth is that in intimate relationships I never said what I needed, *and* I never said what I wanted.)

But that's not entirely true. I told the Tines repeatedly that I wanted to ride on the weekends, and then when she complained about the time I spent on my bike, I ignored my own needs (if I don't ride, I am cray cray) and I didn't ride. When I worked out with my Lesbro on Sunday mornings and the Tines said it ruined our only schedule-free day, I stopped that too. I didn't want relationship strife and felt ill-equipped to handle it, so I sacrificed my own needs. (And, believe me, I understand that by ignoring my own needs, I also undermined our relationship.)

So when things finally and completely blew up with her, I got myself back to the gym and got myself some structure. My mom was dead, and Stef was dead, and the book was launched, and it was time to put myself first.

But I'll tell you, it's hard to do that.

Anything can get in the way of the gym. It's not just a girlfriend or caring for a sick parent. It's my job. It's the weather. It's Facebook. It's that I'm tired. Really, there are a hundred reasons for talking myself out of the gym. My guess is that it was me rather than the Tines who kept me from my bike.

Part of it has to do with long-term motivation. Whether you are listening to yourself, your girlfriend, or the media, "tomorrow, and tomorrow, and tomorrow, creeps in this petty pace" and so why worry about quad strength at sixty-five when you are only fifty-one. And how can a bite-sized salty sweet donut from Mix in Ashland, Oregon, really matter that much in the grand scheme of things, especially when you had the Agave Power Lunch of greens, pepitas, jicama, and grilled chicken? It's hard to keep in mind that the extra glass of wine or the dessert or the cream of artichoke soup can truly change the trajectory of a life. But I've seen in my own life that, indeed, it can. And I watched it happened with both my parents.

Yet when it is sunny and you are sitting on the plaza in Ashland, Oregon, drinking a dairy-free latte (you can't throw every habit out the window!) and you just want a lovely little pastry something to go with it, well, there's the challenge—remembering the trajectory of your life. Remembering that you feel physically and psychically better in size M than size XL—even though you shouldn't judge yourself by the label in the back of your shorts or your shirts.

That's why you need short-term goals too. Like fitting comfortably into your suit for the Oregon Book Awards or your tuxedo for the Lammys. Do you remember that 24 Hour Fitness television commercial that showed people in group exercise classes wearing different T-shirts emblazoned with the reasons they were working out? One of those T-shirts said, "To look good naked." That's also a good reason to go to the gym, to choose the banana over the banana bread.

And then at some point, being an athlete became more important than all of these reasons. The endorphin rush I get when I do eight perfect pushups in a row or back squat 110 pounds became its own reward. I learned from other midlife athletes that just because I wasn't a jock in high school doesn't make me any less an athlete now. Felicity Aston, an Arctic explorer says, "Success or failure has more to do with what is going on in your head than the size of your muscles. . . . If you have an ambition the most important thing you have to do is to start on your journey towards making it happen. Then it's just a matter of perseverance."

In July 2015 I was goblet squatting my body weight.

Now I'm squatting my body weight plus a barbell loaded with 110 extra pounds. And along the way, I regained my faith in myself, my belief in the knowledge that tiny steps accrete and suddenly I'm farther down the road, quite literally, riding my bike for forty-five miles and then going on with the rest of my day. Have I lost all of those thirty-five pounds I gained by eating dates—did you know each date is a hundred calories? Jesus, that's like half a package of M&Ms—and gluten-free chocolate cake kindly delivered by my mother's caregivers? No. But I'm on my way.

CLOTHES MAKE THE BOI

Six years ago I saw *Hamlet* at the Oregon Shakespeare Festival (OSF) in Ashland, just a month after my dad died. I was there with the woman I thought was going to be my next wife, my final wife, actually, and with her family who had been attending plays at OSF since the seventies.

This *Hamlet* was different from any other I'd seen before—and with undergrad and graduate degrees in English, I've seen my fair share, including a BBC recording of Laurence Olivier playing the Dane on a West End stage (the version I liked the least, by the way). But this OSF version rocked my world. Maybe because my own father had just died, and I swear to you that while I didn't see his ghost, I did receive an uncanny, otherworldly message from him letting me know he was all right. So, I understood Hamlet in an entirely new way: his grief, his obsession, his confusion, his longing for more contact with the other side.

What I didn't know is that Hamlet dresses the way he does, in "suits of solemn black," because he's searching for something, anything to express his grief and anguish—although he believes that nothing can truly "denote" what he's feeling. Still, Polonius goes on to say, "Spend all you can afford on clothes, but make sure they're quality, not flashy, since clothes make the man—which is doubly true in France."

I'm pretty sure it's doubly true in New York City too, which is where I'll be in one of my father's tuxedos for the Twenty-Eighth Lambda Literary Awards. It's actually a really beautiful thing. Although he had no need for these after he retired, the tuxedos and two other suits—all size 50-regular—were the ones my father kept and were the ones I took for myself when I cleaned out my parents' house after he died.

I wear a 40-short slim-cut suit, so remaking these tuxedos to fit me was no easy task, but it still cost less than buying new ones, and I got two for about half the price of a new one. There is something so incredibly satisfying in slipping on his suit. Satisfying because he appreciated fine clothes just as much as I do. Satisfying because he spent years hurling invectives against me and my sexuality and my gender presentation, and now I was remaking, quite literally, that pain. Satisfying because right before he died, and I weighed thirty pounds more, I walked into his hospital room wearing one of his vests (fitting into it just fine then), and he smiled and bade me to come near so he could adjust the silk tie across the back.

He said, "You look good in that." It was a blessing, really, an asking of forgiveness in a single statement. An understanding that for all that we'd said in anger, nothing mattered now, and that I was taking his place as the head of the family, in some of the very clothes he'd worn, and that it would be okay. Was okay. Is okay. When you've felt wrong in clothes your whole life, to come to the right clothing in your late forties is such a relief. I have searched for metaphors to describe this, and the best I have actually comes from *Objects In Mirror Are Closer Than They Appear* (with slight changes here for context):

> This is how it feels to wear the right clothes: it is like diving into a cool, mineral-laden river, the way water slides all silky over skin turned pink from too much July sun, the way a body moves with the current—slipping along seemingly languidly only to find itself much farther downstream than expected.

Or it feels like this: like a sigh made at the end of a long day when at last you can crawl into your king-sized bed just made with clean, purple 600 thread count Egyptian cotton sheets—like a whisper across your tired body—the memory foam mattress a reminder of what soft is supposed to feel like.

It does not feel like sitting exposed on top of a white rock mesa in New Mexico's Chaco Canyon, the wind kicking up the fine grit of desert topsoil and the pulverized sandstone exfoliating the fair Irish skin on my cheeks and neck, searing my eyes, worrying my chattering mind about melanomas and carcinomas and survival in this too-bright landscape. No, that's what dresses, skirts, and silk shirts—complete with pushup bras and pearls—feel like.

I feel handsome not beautiful, dapper not sexy. Of course tuxedo rather than dress. Of course bow tie rather than pearls.

As you walk into the Lambda Literary Awards, they snap your photograph on a red carpet, just like at the Academy Awards or the Grammys. And so when I step onto the red carpet at the Skirball Center for the Performing Arts at NYU, I'll be sporting a black shawl-collar tuxedo, red tie, red suspenders, and the hottest saddle shoes you've ever seen. I'll be there with my amazing chosen family: the Ironman, the Sailor, my Lesbro, and one of the Coffee Girls (and she'll be in a complementary colored dress, hanging off my arm as my date for the evening). I'll be laughing and feeling entirely like myself—which makes me a winner whether I walk home with a book award or not.

JUST BREATHE NORMALLY

Facebook just reminded me that in July 2015, I started writing *The Authenticity Experiment*. I began it as a thirty-day challenge because I believe that a culture that consistently ignores its dark winds up like, well, like we are, where we are hap, hap, HAPPY all the time and we get our dark out by watching reality TV (or violent movies) and snarking on grammar signs at the DMV (not that good grammar isn't important). I wrote every day for thirty days, even as my mom suffered multiple strokes and began actively dying. Even as my sister Sue and I were forced by the administration at my mother's assisted living facility to move her to a new home just ten days before she died because the first place didn't want a death on its books. (Even as the summer literally heated up to weeks of ninety-plus degrees, I kept writing in my un-air-conditioned condo. Each night I'd sit on the couch and type out a post, which was unusual for me because I do my creative work longhand. In fact, all of *Objects In Mirror Are Closer Than They Appear* was written in Moleskine journals with fountain pens. But the *Authenticity Experiment* has always been written electronically.)

Now I am a Rain Man with dates even without Facebook reminding me, but I can tell you that the "On This Day" feature of Facebook reminds me of even more things—things I'd often sooner forget. I would not have remembered, for instance, that in July 2012 I was in a similar inferno, wracked with anxiety, left a few weeks earlier by the Opera Singer, and driving to California to rest in the circle of my oldest friends and to stay a few days with my former in-laws (as if we could still maintain a relationship—I've learned a bit about boundaries since then). But Facebook reminded me of this trip, telling me that I posted, "Hello, Redding.

Dear gods yer hot." A funny post that let my family and friends know *where* I was, but not *how* I was.

Two hours after that, I was in a rest stop outside of Dunnigan, California, (Bill and Kathy's sadly closed, for those of you familiar with the I-5 and 505 interchange) in my packed Kia Soul. I was ruined with anxiety. And when I say *ruined*, I mean in a car, in hundred-degree weather, with all the windows rolled up, sobbing and crouched in the passenger's seat rocking and waiting for the Ativan to take effect. I had—I still have—a handbook for sanity that I'd created. One of the things in it was a list of people I could call when I freaked out. I called nine people on that list and nine voicemails answered my call. Clearly, self-rescue was the only option here.

Before I tell you what happened next, let me say I'd spent most of my adult life smug that I'd never needed anti-anxiety meds—especially because I come from nervous people. My grandmother took the earliest of anti-anxiety meds, phenobarbital, and then when Valium came out in the sixties, she started taking that. Her oldest sister, Bobby, first snapped—anxiously speaking—at twenty, which would have been in 1915. I'm not sure if there was anything other than Lydia Pinkham's Elixir to help Bobby, so instead, her parents put her on a slow boat to Europe as a "cure." (As an aside, I'm pretty sure I would never need another Ativan if someone put me on a slow boat to Europe as a cure. I'm just saying.) My mother and father also needed anti-anxiety meds, and my sisters are not opposed to the occasional Ativan themselves. Like I said, my people are nervous.

For me, not taking Ativan or Xanax or Valium or Klonopin was like earning a reverse Girl Scout badge—the Coping through Hard Times by Your Own Wits badge. The Suck It Up Buttercup badge. The Fuck You I Don't Need

Any of You People or Your Pity badge. I thought *not* using these meds made me tough, tougher, more of a survivor. Even though my ex-wife and my Designer Gay love to tell the story about me fainting in a mop closet in the back of a coffee shop in the Clackamas Town Center, knees buckling, edges of the world going black because I felt certain there wasn't enough oxygen in the tiny space. (I was twenty-three.) Or fainting on a Pan Am 747 flying from Sea-Tac to SFO, a little easier because the seat cradled me as my head lolled back, then fell forward to my chest. (Again, a "lack" of oxygen.)

If you meet me in the real world, you know that I talk a lot about anxiety and Ativan. I talk about it because I think many more of us are anxious than not. Many more of us are assaulted by the digital information overload than not. Many of us worry—about oxygen (or the lack thereof), about money (or the lack thereof), about crime, about the Orange Jesus, about antibiotic-resistant bacteria, about our weight, about our fame (or lack thereof), about our legacy (you know what I'm going to say here), about, about, about. I think we need a more public conversation about our fears and the physical responses we have to them, and I'm happy to be the one doing it. But, apparently, I talk so much about anxiety and Ativan that a woman with whom I went on three dates accused me of being addicted to it.

Lest you worry too, you should know that I need Ativan maybe once a month. I have learned that huge public speaking events—like the Oregon Book Awards or the Lambda Literary Awards—require me to take 0.25 mg of Ativan, half of the smallest dose they make, so that I don't lisp if I have to speak and so that I stay firmly grounded in my body. If you go on YouTube and watch the videos from the OBAs or the Lammys, you'll see that in each, at the beginning, there is a moment when I grab the podium with my right hand because I am unsteady. Not quite on the verge of fainting but starting to spin up. Who knows what would happen without that pill melting under my tongue? You know, the Gerding Theater, where the Oregon Book Awards were held, is known to be a low oxygen environment. But at parties or casual reading events? I'm typically fine without the chip of calm.

What Ativan did for me in that hot car in the rest area was let me take a step back from my fears and anxieties. It allowed me to realize that I was not *actually* crazy, I was just *feeling* crazy. By calming down my nervous system, it let my executive function take over and reason with myself. That reasoning included getting out of the car and walking through the grove of eucalyptus trees that borders the rest area until I felt grounded and then driving myself to the nearest nice hotel, cranking the AC, stretching out under clean sheets, and watching six hours of cable television, thinking about virtually nothing. The next morning, I got up, found a gym, worked out, and drove to the Russian River where I met my oldest friends. No Ativan required.

I started this essay thinking about dates and my Rain Man–like ability to remember what happened when and—before perimenopause—who said what and where they were standing in the room when they said it. I think my ability to remember when, where, and what are directly connected to feeling a need for control—and isn't that just what anxiety is too? At least mine? Feeling like the world is out of control? Or I'm out of control in the world? Or both. Especially now with all the ways we have to get information and contact each other.

That's what my emergency handbook is: a way to be in contact with the world. *Real live contact with real live people.*

And I think that's why the *Authenticity Experiment* essays still work. It's about the foibles and struggles of a real live person learning what she can and cannot control. It's not pictures of risotto and sunsets augmented by Pixlr. It's not curated. It's unexpurgated, in fact. There's anxiety, and grief, and love, and heartache, and all of it happening each and every day, multiple times a day, all at once. Because this is life, people. Let's live it completely. Life is nothing but duality, both/and, light/dark, good/bad.

ON COMPASSION

Tonight I had dinner with old friends, the Blonde Bombshell and her Sportscaster wife. They drove up to St. John's to eat on the main square, and we spent two and a half hours talking and laughing, covering everything from the transcendent (shamans and somatic experience) to the mundane (how do you get away from someone in a tiny house?).

Twenty-one years ago, the Bombshell and I worked together at the only truly corporate job I ever had. At the time, she was married to a man and I was married to my ex-wife. But I suspected the Bombshell was gay because one day I caught her looking at my calves. It wasn't until years later that she told me she'd had a terrible crush on me. She said it again tonight, "Oh, I had such a crush on you then."

I still don't know what to make of this information. A six-foot tall blonde bombshell. How could she possibly have been interested in me? This is a persistent problem in my life, self-worth. It's a persistent problem in all our lives, I believe—how do we cultivate self-worth, certainly, but even more so, how do we cultivate self-compassion? How do we find the kindness within that lets us accept that even though we were overweight and dressed in XXL clothes to "hide" our girth, someone still had a crush on us?

One of my heroes, Krista Tippett, hosts a show called *On Being*. I've listened to it for thirteen years, even back when it was called *Speaking of Faith* and I was afraid it was a sneaky liberal way to bring me to. Tippett talks often of compassion. Here's a quote: "Our culture is obsessed with perfection and with hiding problems. But what a liberating thing to realize that our problems, in fact, are probably our richest sources for rising to this ultimate virtue of compassion. . . . Compassion can be synonymous with empathy. It can be joined with the harder work of forgiveness and reconciliation. But it can also express itself in the simple act of presence. It's linked to practical virtues like generosity and hospitality and just being there—just showing up."

How often do we show up for ourselves? I'd argue that as rampant as narcissism is in this culture, we don't very often show up for ourselves in the way Tippett posits: in a kind, curious, generous way. Two summers ago when it became apparent that my mom was going downhill quickly and I couldn't yet get her to agree to change real estate agents so we could get her house sold, I was spending a lot of time driving between Portland and the Olympic Peninsula. I was tired and jagged, there was no time for me, and instead of realizing it, I just beat the shit out of myself for failing to get my workouts in, failing to eat right, failing to show up for my girlfriend. Then a veritable stranger said to me, "Geesh, you're managing so much! Do you ever just stop, take three deep breaths, put your hand on your forehead, and talk nicely to yourself? You should try it. It's really comforting."

Funny thing is, I did what she said, and then I immediately started to cry. I *was* managing a lot. I *am still* managing a lot, and this practice has become for me a daily reminder to treat myself with the same compassion I reserve for others, to show up for myself in the same way I'd show up for others. It's hard to be in the world. We can make it easier by being nicer to ourselves—and then that kindness ripples outward. Tonight three friends showed up for each other—but we showed up for ourselves as well, talking gently about fears and foibles, laughing and sitting outside in the gloaming while the light grew within.

TAKE ME TO CHURCH

When I was in Amsterdam, I visited a hidden Catholic church, "Our Lord in the Attic," built into the top two floors of a classic Amsterdam row house. The church was built more than forty years after the 1578 Alteration when the Netherlands outlawed Catholicism, sent the priests packing, and turned the churches over to the Calvinists. So the Catholics practiced in secret, in hidden spaces.

For years gay bars were my church. The one place where I could let out a full exhale. I didn't even know that I was holding my breath, holding tension in my body, until I'd walk into the Primary Domain or the 927 in Portland, Oregon, or Amelia's in San Francisco's Mission or Café San Marco in the Castro, and suddenly this great rush of an exhale would leave my body and my shoulders would drop a little lower, and I wouldn't feel so guarded. Because here were my people. Here it was safe to hold my wife's hand. Here we could kiss and dance and laugh and be our full selves without hiding. Here I could worship—myself, others. The bulldaggers who scared me. The queens who amused me. The femmes who flustered me. The leathermen who strangely aroused me.

And like that church in Amsterdam, these bars were hidden away, very often without a window facing the street. Just a nondescript door, nothing written on it, often no address—even in places like San Francisco. You had to know where to go, where to worship. The Rawhide, a great country western bar, was just a gray door on Seventh Street, south of Market. No place "nice" people went in the seventies and eighties.

I remember going into the Rawhide the very first time. I was nervous because the entrance was so dark. Even today, gay bars are dark when you enter—a hallmark, I suppose, of the years when you didn't want your face lit up as you pulled open a door on some side street. Didn't want to be seen entering. Didn't want the patrons to be visible to anyone passing by on the street. Didn't want to expose anyone—yourself included—to an unnecessary police raid (you know, besides the raids the bar owners and police planned for every month).

In the eighties, Seventh Street, South of Market, was not the gentrified, yuppified, chic neighborhood you see today. It was piss-soaked alleys and drug addicts. MoMA SF not even conceived of. In the eighties, Seventh Street was plastic bags blowing down the sidewalk, broken glass, homeless men, and a gray metal door at 280 Seventh that led into the Rawhide.

I don't know why it was that I was alone there. Perhaps, home for Christmas, I bailed on my family for a few hours of bar time, heading to a place where I felt seen and normal. All I remember is that I was leaning back against a bar, resting my elbows like some dyke version of the Marlboro Man, a long-necked Budweiser in my left hand, my right hooked into the pocket of my Levi's.

The story I told myself was that I couldn't dance. And I couldn't, at least not then. Certainly not country two-step. (The Opera Singer, an expert from her years of living in Jackson, taught me that in our living room.) So when a beautiful, tall, long-haired femme came up to me and asked if I could two-step, I grinned, touched my right hand to my heart and said, "No, but you make me wish I could." It was a bold move for someone who didn't feel attractive, didn't believe that any woman ever noticed her. But this woman did, and I've never forgotten her. Of course, I've always been a sucker for a girl who can fix fence and then dance backward in cowboy boots.

As I remember it, she said, "Oh, such a pity."

Yes. Such a pity.

But not a tragedy. Not like Orlando. Orlando, where the young twenty- and thirty-somethings were dancing salsa and merengue, where the young queer kids and trans kids— and I'm an elder now, if only by the mandate of my gray hair, so they were *kids* to me—were exhaling and inhaling, allowed for an evening to be their whole selves. No hiding. Worshipping in the best way they—we all—know how. Worshipping in the way I think the gods intended, by dancing and laughing. A Tweet by @jerameykraatz that went viral said, "If you can't wrap your head around a bar or a club as a sanctuary, you've probably never been afraid to hold someone's hand in public." I have. I sometimes still am. I will always be aware—even in the liberal bubble of #Portlandia—of when it is safe to touch or kiss, and when it is not.

∞

So many things make me angry about Orlando. So many things. But perhaps the worst are the politicians who vote to deny us protections, who use us as political fodder for their culture war, perpetuating homophobia, and then refuse to call this a hate crime. Because they can villainize the shooter as a Muslim and fan the flames of Islamophobia and the fears of terrorism. To the politicians, Orlando isn't a hate crime to kick off Pride month. It's terrorism that cut down the lives of "Americans." Brown and black Americans who would otherwise be called undocumented workers or homosexuals, faggots and dykes who steal jobs from hard working white people, are suddenly "American victims of terrorism."

You can't have it both ways, people.

And to the straight people who have remained silent because you are uncertain of what to say—and that includes every single client of mine save one—say something, say anything, even if it is ham-handed. Acknowledge, as one of my friends said, that this is our 9/11. The shooter was not some radicalized Muslim. He was a man who hated queers because he hated himself. This is a hate crime. Don't make it worse by staying silent. Silence is the voice of complicity.

Let me say that again: this is a hate crime. Don't make it worse by staying silent.

Every June Portland erupts for our Pride weekend. There's the Trans Parade, the Dyke March, and the Pride Parade proper. Are we scared? Yes. Will we let this fear stop us? It hasn't yet. It won't now. But we'll have backup plans and be on guard. Maybe you could show up and have our backs too.

WIPING CLEAN REGRET

For the first six months after my father died, I'd say to the Opera Singer, "My dad is dead." She would pat me on the leg and say, "Yes. It's so sad." I'd lean my head against her, breathe into the loss, then, just as quickly continue on with whatever it was I had been doing. The patting, the leaning, it was a very animal/sensate thing to do, and it helped me get it in my body—metabolize the shock of loss.

When your parent dies, when a beloved dies, you are wracked with guilt and what-ifs. I don't care if you are a Jungian analyst who seems entirely together or someone who has never really done any therapy. Death makes us feel regret. But the Opera Singer stopped me from doing this— reminded me again and again how dangerous it was to entertain regret, let alone invite it in and cook it dinner. She'd shake her head, call me her pet name, and tell me not to start. Gently, kindly, but fiercely, too, because she knew the dark places my mind could take me. It was a good lesson that I've carried forward.

My mom died ten months ago. And the brain, it wants to wander into the weeds of persecution. Mostly now, I'm good at stopping myself—especially when it comes to wondering and worrying about the choices I made for her care, the decision to keep managing things (because I had to, honestly) rather than simply sit on the couch and join her in her ennui and confusion.

But one thing nags at me so. For as long as I could remember, my mother used Handi Wipes to clean the counter and wash dishes (unless caked-on, baked-on bits covered the dish, in which case a Lola brush would be employed). My sisters, my partner, we all hated the damn Handi Wipes. They smelled and required changing often.

They seemed to just smear water across the counter rather than really clean it. And their relative skimpiness made cleaning challenging for all but the most transient food scraps.

Still, my mother had likely cleaned her kitchen with Handi Wipes since the seventies. I never remember a kitchen without them. But when we moved her to assisted living, we didn't bring them—even though my parents' pantry overflowed with the blue-and-white-striped cloths. Thanks to my father's little Costco addiction, my parents had enough Handi Wipes, Comet, 409, and Ziploc bags to last through the zombie apocalypse. But we sold all those items in the estate sale. Partly, I think, because my mom was supposed to eat her meals in the assisted living dining room and partly because we were snarky kids who thought we knew better. After the move, I put a nice, blue Ocelo sponge on the top left edge of the sink. A sponge you could microwave to kill germs. A sponge with a built-in scrubber. A sponge that held soap.

She asked me a couple of times for some Handi Wipes. Turns out that the Clorox Company bought the Handi Wipe Company and then discontinued the iconic stripped rags. Suddenly, I felt frantic for the thin, stretchy cloths. I ordered some from Amazon (repository of all things) and when they came, I threw them in the trunk of my mom's car, intending to bring them up to her apartment. But they disappeared into the cavernous back, and tasks like the neurologist, the cardiologist, shopping, and socialization took precedence. It bugged me, though, because they'd been there in the car, and then they weren't. But it didn't bug me enough to reorder them.

A few months before she died, I sold the car that she'd given up. I didn't tell her because not driving felt like such a defeat, such a prison sentence. I just couldn't see traumatizing her more by telling her I'd let the car go for $4,500—which was, synchronistically, the same cost as a month of her care. As I cleaned out the back of the car, I noticed something jammed between the seat and the trunk: the Handi Wipes. They'd slid between the two compartments when I'd had the seat down.

By now, though, it was too late. My mom had stopped going into her kitchen at all, even though her entire apartment was only 550 square feet. Twice a week, I soaped up the soft side of the blue sponge to wash the coffee cups and water glasses that aides filled for her, and used the rough side to scrub the silverware with which she picked at her meals.

And when I cleaned out her apartment after she'd died, I sent the package of Handi Wipes to Goodwill.

CAME TO BELIEVE

Here is a scene: nighttime, the only light coming into my periwinkle blue office is from the streetlight on the corner of Southeast Thirty-Eighth Street and Southeast Washington Street. If I look out the window to the west, I can see the radio towers across town, on the top of Skyline Drive, winking on and off, sending their music and news and messages over the region. You and I are sitting quietly in here. I can no longer remember why. I believe that this is pre-heart-surgery, but how do I know this, really? I don't. It's more a sense because of how I remember you sitting in the oak liberty-back chair, the seat pressed up against the low windowsill, your right elbow resting on the desk my father purchased for me during my sophomore year of college—now my wife's desk—the file drawers full of vinyl photo-pocket sheets categorizing not pictures, but the Chinese herbs she is studying for her master's degree. The office always smelled of the herbs, a scent originally disconcerting but which I grew to love because I associated it with my wife's flight into her new career. So that's why I think this night was some time before 2004, sometime before my wife was licensed, and the herbs left the office. Also, in my memory I don't hear the hiss of the Wound Vac as it decompresses and then the tiny motor kicking on as it begins sucking, pulling the colloidal silver-impregnated sponge tight against your chest walls, blown open by heart surgery gone wrong.

This night I'm remembering, I'd swiveled in my blue Herman Miller Aeron chair—maybe the dot com had not yet even crashed—to face your profile. As I look back, I can see you crying. You never cried loudly. Tears just streamed down your cheeks. Until you spoke and I heard your baritone rising up to alto, I never knew anything was out of order. This was how you bore your pain. Silently. Alone. Without much support.

We'd been speaking about my father—that much I have retained. And I remember the questions and answers that came next because I used them later to evaluate my own marriage.

"Why do you stay with him?" I'd asked you.

"I don't know, honey," you said. "I really don't know. After so many years. You just."

And here you stopped for a minute and, I imagine, probably blew your nose. You could not abide mucus— "snot," a word we were not allowed to use, even as adults— coming from your nose or anyone else's.

Then you continued. "It's just sometimes, when your dad is sleeping, I look at him and I see the damaged little boy and my heart breaks."

I'll tell you honestly now. This was fourteen, fifteen, maybe even sixteen years ago. I'd certainly not turned forty, the transit of midlife still an abstract idea, even as I saw my friends in the middle of it. Because of that, I thought your answer was utter bullshit.

Then, then, then. Then within four or five years I'd lost my sainted golden retriever and two cats. Within six or seven years I'd left my own marriage and watched both you and dad have heart attacks and bypasses. I dropped the first fifty pounds of armor I wore. I started graduate school. I fell in love. I lost my dad to esophageal cancer before graduate school ended. And I watched my ex-wife marry her high school boyfriend three times (that's a long story). Basically, what I'm telling you is that the bullshit answer I thought you gave me, there's no way I could have begun to understand it then. Couldn't yet understand the comfort of falling asleep next to your history even when that history was mean, violent, abusive. Couldn't understand the powerful denial processes of the spouses and children of alcoholics, their fervent belief that things will always get better, if only. I mean, that's our American ideal, right? And I couldn't, wouldn't—maybe even refused—to understand this for at least another fifteen years.

Now you're dead and I can't tell you what I've learned from watching two different lovers parent their children. Two different lovers who both have ex-spouses with war-induced PTSD. Ex-spouses who also drink and love guns, who are "wildly" unpredictable (which is, I suppose, the very nature of unpredictability). It's given me new insight into the delicate and complicated dance steps you maneuvered. When you sat on the patio alone on hot summer nights, Dr. Scholl's on the bricks, feet kicked up on the spool table you painted dark brown to match the gutter trim and the benches the neighbor husband built because Dad wouldn't, when you sat there, head resting against the cushion of the chair, looking up at the grape arbor and between the leaves at bits of the Northern California night sky, the fog not yet rolled in, when you sat there alone in the dark smoking Kool cigarette after Kool cigarette, I understand now you were strategizing how best to approach him, how to ensure the family ran smoothly without some unpredicted, unpredictable blowup. You sat there decompressing from the stress of behaving like Oz—one life for us (mostly), and one life going on behind the curtain.

Now, I see how tired you were. I wish I could have learned this sooner. I might have believed you when you told me, "You have no idea how hard I tried to keep you safe from him." I might have given you more grace and compassion. I might have said *I'm sorry* when you still were living. I might have had much more empathy for you that night so long ago. For the way that you felt leaving was really no choice at all: Go, and you've failed and your children don't have a father, something you vowed they would never live without. Stay, and you've failed because you eat your rage until you are not only physically ill, but become predator too, lashing back at Dad with insults as vitriolic as he ever hurled at you.

It's ironic to me, the hypervigilant one, that I never saw all you truly did to protect me from him. But I did see it twice, didn't I? Once when I was twelve and I came around the corner early one summer morning to find you sitting at the kitchen table—the same one I have now—cigarette burning in a grey and blue ceramic ashtray, a pedestal cup full of coffee sitting on a leather coaster you brought back from Mexico City, and you sobbing into a kitchen hand towel. Sobbing harder than I had ever seen or ever did again. Twelve going on thirteen, I looked so gay then, right? That's the year things shift for most girls—Maybelline blue eyeshadow, Bonnie Bell Lip Smackers, nylons, and platform heels—shifted for my friends, but not for me. I'll never know why you cried so hard that early morning, but the story I tell myself now was that you had been fighting with Dad about your butch daughter.

Then, the other time, I'd already left my ex-wife, so there was no third party to cut the tension. Dad and I were fighting in the family room in Sequim. Again, who knows why? Maybe because he wanted me to clean the gutters, or caulk the vents, or string trim the front yard (a cool quarter of an acre). The argument began at the table. (Really, why did I take that table?) Initially, you yelled back at him.

I raised my hand and said, "Let me have my own relationship with Dad."

You whipped your walker into the kitchen—in a fury—to clean the dinner mess: load the plates, wash the pans. Dad and I continued arguing, hard now—I cannot remember the words or the topic. I can only remember how it felt in my body, edge of nausea as I write this, pecs contracting, brow furrowing. And you in the kitchen grabbed two pot lids and banged them together like cymbals, a domestic Harold Hill. You looked at me over your right shoulder and you smirked. I held my hand up again, shook my head, gave you the slightest smile and said, "I got this, thank you."

I was at least forty-two. Nine years later, I see that even then you were still trying to keep me away from the full force of my father's rage. And though you're dead, I hope you can hear me when I say, "Now I have an idea of what you did. Thank you for keeping me as safe as you knew how to do. I'm sorry I couldn't appreciate this earlier. And I'm also sorry you didn't leave and get the life you deserved."

REMEMBER?

I don't even know where to start. That's the prompt that the Woman Who Is Not My Girlfriend threw at me on a Sunday night when I told her I was blocked. She said, "Start with 'I don't even know where to start.' And then give me two pages by morning." She laughed her big laugh, head thrown back and white teeth shining in the light of a beach fire, and continued, "That's what you'd say to me. Two pages by morning." There was pure delight in that laugh, in the turnabout.

I thought both *touché* and *fuck off* because she was right. I don't know where to start. The truth is, I don't want to start. Because I'm scared. Because it's painful. Because my mother has only been dead ten months and one week and maybe it's too soon. Because fuck all, I am trying to get over death, not relive it.

And so I didn't write. For all the reasons I just said and because I hate to be told what to do and just because I might feel the tiniest bit stubborn about writing suggestions that feel like therapy suggestions. Also, I'd agreed to a challenge with my writing friend Brenda Miller and a few others. We were to write from a prompt each day for the month of July. It seemed serendipitous because it was on July 20, 2015, that I challenged myself to the *Authenticity Experiment* and now here it was summer 2016, and there was another writing challenge—not an Alzheimer's challenge, oh by the way.

Five of us were completing this challenge, each of us sending the rest of the group a prompt every fifth day. We wrote to the prompts each morning and sent the work in the evening, all very writerly. One of Brenda's pieces arrived in my inbox. She's been writing about her father and the health challenges he's facing. He's in a skilled nursing facility—a nursing home to the layperson—and Brenda is learning how to dance the steps to the role-reversal tango.

One of the paragraphs she wrote said: "*A canary?* I said. I've learned not to contradict him, but to simply nod inquisitively. *Did it sing?* It did not sing, he says. Maybe a pet bird that escaped? *What's the word for those birds,* he asks, *the ones in a cage?* I pause, think back to the house he left behind in Arizona. *Parakeets?* I say, and he nods, smiles a close-lipped smile."

That did it. That line, "I've learned not to contradict him, but to simply nod inquisitively." I tried not to contradict my mother—all the crazy stories floating around in her head. There was no reason to reorient her to the idea that she sometimes believed my sisters and I never called. "Where have you been? I haven't talked to you in weeks!" she'd say, her inflection rising toward hyperbole.

And I'd say, "I just talked to you yesterday after my bike ride, remember?" Which was a mistake. She didn't remember, and that one word—*remember*—just drove home the point and also made her paranoid, made her think I was gaslighting her. Instead, I learned to say, "You must feel really lonely, huh, Mom?" Then she'd cry and, if I was visiting, I'd hold her hand until her brain forgot what she was crying about.

There was no point in arguing that she didn't know where she was in the city or in what city sometimes. She had a map that showed her house, my house, my ex-wife's house, the Tines's house, Stef's house. All places she'd been. All places she knew. Lines drawn between them so she could see that she was at the apex of a big diamond and that anybody could get to her in twenty minutes. But she'd cry and say, "But where is this building in space? I want to go outside and walk around it so I understand where it is in space."

And I would say, "Mom, it sounds like you don't know where home is."

And she would cry and cry and cry and say, "Oh, Katie, I don't. I don't know where home is anymore. Sometimes I think my mother is going to come in the door and fix me breakfast. I hear her talking in the next room, and I don't understand why she's letting me go hungry."

That one always killed me. I didn't reorient her or contradict her on that either. I didn't tell her that my grandmother, her mother, had been dead for thirty-one years. Instead, I said, "I think Grandma is involved in dealing with Dacie. I bet she just lost track of time. How about I fix you some cheese and crackers?"

She would reply in this small, sad voice that broke my heart right open, "Oh that would be so nice. You're always so nice to me."

Dacie had Alzheimer's, too, so that line made sense to my mom, even as it scares the hell out of me. Dacie was my grandmother's sister. Alzheimer's at fifty-four. My mother definitely showed signs of Alzheimer's by sixty-five. I'm fifty-one. This weekend I couldn't remember most of the stories that the Californian told about when we were on tour together. Admittedly, we were last on tour together thirty-five years ago. But you'd think I'd remember the lightning storm in South Dakota, a storm the Californian described in such detail.

Instead, here is what I remember about the same South Dakota town that the Californian presumably described: the glow of the red, white, and blue Amoco sign shining over the gas station that sold an eighteen-year-old kid six silver cans of Bud Light. I remember sitting on a dark, empty stage, directly under the proscenium, drinking the beer, and figuring out a love song: *Is it okay if I call you mine, just for a time? And I will be just fine. If I know that you know that I'm wanting, needing your love.*

But I do not remember sitting on a couch the Californian said that we pulled onto the porch of the community hall we were crashing in. Don't recall sitting there and watching the lightning illuminate the clouds and dark trees of the road leading to Mount Rushmore, even though I said that I did. I just nodded inquisitively until the Californian revealed more of the story that I did remember—how the bus couldn't make it up the switchbacks leading to the Mount Rushmore parking lot and how I've yet to see those granite faces. And then I felt the vaguest of memories in the back of my brain, of rain falling so hard that it obscured the Amoco sign, but maybe that was just later—after a six-pack of Bud Light—which would do the same thing.

I called the Woman Who Is Not My Girlfriend and asked her to assure me I didn't have Alzheimer's. She didn't laugh. She said calmly, "You do not have Alzheimer's. Memory is tricky. You remember the stage. Your friend remembers the couch. Both memories could be true. You remember what's significant for you."

I had to believe her.

On Tuesday I went to breakfast with the Californian before she left town, and I was reminding her of a night in Providence, Rhode Island, when we slept in the attic of a clearly haunted house, and our host locked us into said attic. I know this story is true because I have a journal entry about it. But the Californian remembered nothing of it. So today, just for this moment, I don't think I have Alzheimer's. I think memory is tricky, which is why it's still scary to begin, but if you don't get the thoughts down, they might just get

UNCOVERING THE MIRRORS

In twenty-one days it will have been one year since my mom died. It's almost as if my psyche knows it's time to take off the black armband and uncover the mirrors. I think because of this I'm having trouble writing these essays because I am just far enough removed from my grief that I am not compelled to drop it onto the page every week.

Or maybe it's that I started taking an antidepressant. That's not something I'd normally share (even though I'll tell you all about my anxiety and Ativan, somehow this feels more personal). The truth is, my mother spent much of her life depressed and not doing anything about it, and I realized that I'd fallen into the same pattern, moving myself forward via sheer will but starting to lose focus, lose concentration at work, nap in the middle of the day. Part of this is because I have a new client and I have a 7:30 call every single morning when I used to go to the gym and write. I think my brain chemistry changed because of this—because the endorphins from lifting weights and riding helped keep some of the depression at bay. But now I'm not getting to the gym until the afternoon, which is problematic. But I worry that the drugs will blunt my creativity. Maybe that's why I have been unable to write an essay.

Or maybe it's that during July I did a writing-prompt-a-day challenge with four other writers and that push really sucked the creativity out of me—in a good way—and the fields are now fallow, as fields must sometimes be. Or maybe it's that I really just want to sit on my balcony and do a crossword puzzle and be quiet because it's the middle of summer and the twilight lasts until after nine. Or that I had a six-day road trip with the Alaskan Poet. The Alaskan Poet and I initially bonded deeply over death. Her mother, father, and dog all died within about eight months of each other. My mentor, best friend, and mother all died within ten months. The death has continued in both our lives, and we struggle to understand it. It's not just that we're both in our fifties, we think. Something is going on here. Conspiracy? I dunno. Some weird god that is forcing us to sit still and feel our feelings? Maybe.

But the interesting thing is, grieving is done alone. I mean, the really deep grieving. It's when you're floating solo in a kayak on Scappoose Bay or the Deschutes River. It's when you're wandering along the beach of Kachemak Bay looking at the mountains or you're weeding the garden after dinner in the never-ending Alaskan twilight. And yet, this very human thing—grieving—connects the Alaskan Poet and me, connects all of us together, even as we need vast swaths of time alone to navigate the surprising shoals and eddies of grief.

Yet here we were, the Alaskan Poet and I, together in real life, strapped into a tiny Kia Soul (bikes, guitars, luggage, cans of salmon—because all Alaskans, the Alaskan Poet notwithstanding, always arrive bearing gifts—random snacks, including kombucha, which the Alaskan Poet cannot pronounce but discovered she loved), two introverts driving hundreds and hundreds of miles together from Portland, Oregon, to Whidbey Island, Washington, back down to the Long Beach Peninsula, meeting and greeting people, having to be "on" with each other and the other people we were meeting and who were hosting us on this semi-work-related road trip.

And so there hasn't been enough time alone, enough time listening to podcasts, enough time just staring at the sky—there hasn't been enough time really since June, since the Lammys. I'm supposed to schedule three

DOWNSHIFTING INTO THE STILL POINT

So the darkness shall be the light,
and the stillness the dancing.
   —T. S. Eliot, "East Coker" from *Four Quartets*

I switched cars with the Ironman and drove her Ford Ranger out to my yurt, located in the Columbia Plateau, away from all the city noise and lights. Although the moon was waxing gibbous this year, the Perseid meteor shower was supposed to be amazing, and so I headed out to the dark and the stillness.

The Ironman's truck is, to put it nicely, rudimentary. It's five on the floor with no power steering, tachometer, radio, or air conditioning. Just a bench seat that sits so close to the steering wheel that the previous owner removed the airbag because, were it to deploy, it would do more damage to the driver than just crashing head-on into another car. So black electrical tape runs across the center of the steering wheel, covering the slit from the air bag extraction. And in lieu of a radio, a big piece of black plastic with a Community Cycling Center sticker sits in the middle of the dashboard.

The mercury recently hit ninety-eight, and here I was again driving this truck with no AC, windows down, hair blasted by hot air (better than no wind at all). A year earlier, my sister Sue and I were moving my mother to the foster home where she would die, and so I drove this truck all over town moving furniture from assisted living, to foster home, to storage, to Goodwill. The morning I drove to my yurt, I sent a selfie to Sue; the loaded truck bed was clearly visible through the wide rear window. I captioned the photo, "Here we go." This is what we said to each other every time we took off with another load. Her response came immediately,

"OMG! Total PTSD! You are even wearing the same shirt."

And I was. Because I bought that shirt the day before my mom had her final big stroke—the one that would cause her to shut down completely—and I love it, even though I remember that the day I first wore it, I frantically struggled to hire help for my mother, who lay, more or less unconscious, in the bed my great-grandfather was born and died in (well, okay, we changed the mattress, people, it was just the bed frame). Sue says I'd be a lot happier if I "weren't like Rain Man with the dates." She's right, of course, but I'd like to point out that she's the one who remembered what shirt I wore the first time we were driving around in the truck.

But this truck. There is something supremely simple about just driving. No music, no conversation, downshifting the four-banger to stop the speed loss as you climb up into Hood River, the wind making Bluetooth conversation or streaming music impossible. Nothing but you and your thoughts in a truck like this. Well, you, your thoughts, and a shirt wet with sweat where your back rests against the gray vinyl bench seat.

It had been a long time since I'd driven to the yurt in such a disconnected way. Nine years, in fact. The last time I drove out to Goldendale in a vehicle with no AC, I thought my marriage was ending, and I headed out there for a weekend alone to try and figure out if it was really true. That time I drove the Dudes' blue Jeep Wrangler because my own Ford Ranger—no airbag and no AC but with the relative luxury of an extended cab and captain's chairs—didn't have current tags. The woman that I refer to as my first girlfriend drove a burgundy Jeep CJ7, and I think there was something psychological about driving the Dudes' Wrangler then, driving it at year twenty-three of my marriage. Twenty-three, about the same age as a college graduate leaving home for good.

I could have taken my truck with the expired tags; I'd been driving for months that way. Or I could have driven my wife's Prius. But I took the Jeep. I wanted the wildness of it. I wanted the connection with my youth, I think. The connection with my younger gay self who used to run around in that Jeep CJ7. I wanted a vehicle that could not distract me with bells and whistles—even if those bells and whistles were only a cassette player blasting Ani DiFranco's "Shameless."

My own Ranger, the Dudes' Jeep, the Ironman's Ranger, all had manual transmissions. There is something so satisfying about doing your own shifting—first to second, second to third, third to fourth, and up to fifth at sixty miles per hour. For those of us who learned to drive on manual vehicles, a muscle memory remains—that sweet spot you can hold in first gear where the car isn't moving forward and isn't rolling backward, the sound of 3,000 rpm and then the lack of engine whine as you depress the clutch and shift gears, the satisfaction of the gears changing and the drivetrain becoming whole again.

The other great thing about a manual transmission vehicle and, in particular, the Ironman's manual transmission truck, is that because there is no power steering and the windows are blasting you at sixty miles per hour, you can't hear your phone beep and you certainly can't pick it up and look at it. This truck requires hands at ten and two just to keep it on the road. It's simple really. A car that is just a car and not a hyper-connected entertainment machine.

I know I'm in the minority, though. An article in the *Wall Street Journal* quoted Clay Voorhees, an associate professor at Michigan State University who studies the attitude of millennials toward cars. He said, "The high of getting the Facebook update outweighs the emotional high of experiencing the G-forces of going around a corner." Which means exactly what I discovered, "Driving a manual is going to make you less able to text or check your phone."

But this is a good thing, I think. It leaves time for wonder, time for letting thoughts float back and forth, or better yet, time for no thought at all. Just ninety-eight degrees, a hot floorboard, a sticky back and damp thighs, and the rising and falling of your own breath in time with the whine of the transmission.

જ

Once I arrived at the edge of my property line, I off-roaded through the dry grass up to the yurt—no paved or gravel drive here—and parked under the big ponderosa that stands sentinel. I dropped down into the pine slatted chairs that still haven't rotted, even though they sit here season after season, until more than fifteen years have now passed. The only noise came from the ticking of the truck engine cooling and the deep hush of the wind in the top of the pines and the midrange rattle the oak leaves made. The kind of quiet that restores my soul.

I turned my cell phone to ultra powersaving mode. This turns a smartphone dumb—capable of only receiving texts and calls. No camera. No Internet. No apps. No games. I kept the phone on because my sisters like to check in on me when I'm out here. Otherwise I would have turned it off completely. I won't lie to you: for the first few hours, the FOMO made me twitch a bit.

Then I remembered a night in 2004 when my ex-wife and I and our friends were out here to watch the meteors. We stepped outside sometime around 11:00 p.m., headlamps blazing, ready to walk down to the meadow and watch the stars. Instead we found ourselves in a whiteout. Not snow, but ash blowing through, obscuring everything like the biggest of big blizzards. We thought perhaps Mount St. Helen's new lava dome had exploded, but we had no way of knowing. In the morning, a neighbor told us that the east winds brought the ash from a fire burning out in Bickleton. The not knowing, it didn't kill us. In fact, it made us speculate and wonder and imagine as we talked late into the night.

This time I had no one to talk to, but that was okay. I sat there and listened to the wind and cries of the various birds—mourning dove, naturally, my favorite—sat there and looked out at the valley and the trees, the shifting light and the stealthy deer, sat there and rested in this natural quiet for a good long while.

Notes

Prologue

> Courtney E. Martin, "Showing Up Whole," *On Being* (blog), September 23, 2016, http://www.onbeing.org/blog/courtney-martin-showing-up-whole-despite-all-the-risks/8948.

The Dark and the Light

> Debbie Ford, *Dark Side of the Light Chasers: Reclaiming Your Power, Creativity, Brilliance, and Dreams* (New York: G.P. Putnam's Sons, 1998), 79.
>
> Marion Woodman in *Marion Woodman: Dancing in the Flames*, DVD, Directed and edited by Adam Greydon Reid. Toronto, Ontario: Capri Vision Films, 2009.

Wish You Were Here

> Seth Godin quoted in Krista Tippett, "Maria Popova: Cartographer of Meaning in a Digital Age," *On Being* (podcast), May 14, 2015. http://www.onbeing.org/program/transcript/7584.

Sitting Alone

> Matthew Brashears et al., "Social Isolation in America: Changes in Core Discussion Networks Over Two Decades," *American Sociological Review* 71 (June 2006), DOI: 10.1177/000312240607100301.

Letting the Words Wash Over You

> Krista Tippett, "Maria Popova: Cartographer of Meaning in a Digital Age," *On Being* (podcast), May 14, 2015. http://www.onbeing.org/program/transcript/7584.

William Wordsworth, "The World Is Too Much
With Us," in *Poems, in Two Volumes* (London: Printed
for Longman, Hurst, Rees, and Orme, 1807).

Here/There, Both/And

Courtney E. Martin, "To See One Another Broken,"
On Being (blog), August 7, 2015,
http://www.onbeing.org/blog/to-see-one-another-
broken/7808.

The History in the Chimney of My Heart

Tom Robbins, *Another Roadside Attraction* (New
York: Bantam, 1991), 122.

I Knew I Knew What I Knew

Judith Kitchen, "Mending Wall," *Seneca Review* 37,
no. 2 (Fall 2007): 45.

Grief Dispatches

Gregory Orr, "[Untitled] Grief Will Come to You,"
in *How Beautiful the Beloved* (Port Townsend, WA:
Copper Canyon Press, 2009), 20.

Tornado Weather

N. R. Kleinfield, "Fraying at the Edges: Her Fight to
Live with Alzheimer's," *New York Times*, April 30,
2016,
http://www.nytimes.com/interactive/2016/05/01/
nyregion/living-with-alzheimers.html.

Instructions for Grieving

Krista Tippett, "David Steindl-Rast: Anatomy of
Gratitude," *On Being* (podcast), January 21, 2015.
http://www.onbeing.org/program/david-steindl-
rast-anatomy-of-gratitude/8361.

The Wreckage

Aaron Fox in "Songs That Cross Borders," *Radiolab*
(podcast), season 4, episode 5.

http://www.radiolab.org/story/91635-songs-that-cross-borders/.

William Wordsworth, "Ode: Intimations of Immortality," in *Poems, in Two Volumes* (London: Printed for Longman, Hurst, Rees, and Orme, 1807).

The Twenty-Ton Shield

Brené Brown,*The Gifts of Imperfection: Let Go of Who You Think You're Supposed to Be and Embrace Who You Are,* (Center City, MN: Hazelden, 2010).

On Softening

Carrie Newcomer, "Three Gratitudes" in *A Permeable Life: Poems & Essays* (Available Light Publishing, 2014)

Don't Think Twice

Brett Duncan, "Remembering Bob Dylan" (blog), http://ideadrenaline.com/remember-bob-dylan/

Much, Much Less

Adyashanti lecture, Alberta Abbey, Portland, Oregon, March 21, 2015

Behind the Curtain

Deb Talan, "Big Strong Girl" ASCAP

Trying to Find Home Again

Joan Didion, "On Going Home," in *Slouching Towards Bethlehem* (New York: Farrar, Straus and Giroux, 1968), 165.

Dear Judith

Judith Kitchen, "The Circus Train" (Port Townsend, WA: Ovenbird Books, 2013), 119.

My Father Was a Dandy

Naomi Wolf, *The Beauty Myth* (New York: Harper Perennial, 1990), 187.

Perseverance

      William Shakespeare, "Macbeth's Speech:
      Tomorrow, and tomorrow, and tomorrow," *Macbeth*,
      act 5, scene 5.

      Felicity Ashton, *Alone in Antarctica: The First Woman*
      to Ski Solo across the Southern Ice (Berkeley, CA:
      Counterpoint Press, 2014).

On Compassion

      Krista Tippett, "Reconnecting with Compassion."
      Filmed November 2010 TEDPrize@UN video,
      15:53.
      https://www.ted.com/talks/krista_tippett_reconne
      cting_with_compassion.

Downshifting into the Still Point

      Zusha Elinson, "Do You Drive Stick? Fans of
      Manual Transmission Can't Let Go," *Wall Street*
      Journal, November 9, 2015,
      http://www.wsj.com/articles/do-you-drive-stick-
      fans-of-manual-transmission-cant-let-go-
      1447120357.

Acknowledgments

I said it with *Objects*, and I'll say it here, too: it takes a village to write a book and get it out the door. And I would be a total mess without my village, not only because they got me writing to begin with—thank you, Fleda Brown for the initial inspiration and Erin Coughlin Hollowell for shouting at me in a loud, dark Irish bar at AWP Minneapolis that a daily writing practice was transformational—but also because my village tribe truly walked with me on this path of grief, celebrating the good, the bad, and the mundane in between.

To my sisters, Sue and Jule: from rats' nests to furniture guarantees, from the back of beyond to the sixth floor of a hot, stagnant storage warehouse on the banks of the Willamette River, from refreshing adult beverages at the end of a day spent cleaning out the storeroom to mimosas and coffee the morning Mom died, we did what had to be done. No essay will ever be able to capture the insanity and the humor of the DeGuti. "Here we go."

To Jen Dole: for being another sister, for always buying tonic and Tanqueray, for making me laugh every single time we're together, and for never complaining when I crash on your living room floor.

To Janice, Jenn, Jill, Kelly, Lynn, and Niki: for showing up and carrying out any and every request. You guys are rock stars (literally).

To Laura: you said it best, "For decades of friendship, often (mostly) completely disconnected and present only in memory, which allowed us to develop an even deeper and better friendship at the five decade marker when, I think—despite all we'd [already] been through before—we really needed each other."

To the dappers and dames: for doing turn out, showing up to readings, serving as flying wedges, introducing me to the best bourbon yet, and embracing me so I didn't feel so conspicuous or alone, and always making me laugh, thank you.

Huge thanks to the crew who read this in manuscript form and offered such constructive feedback: Julie Harrelson, Erin Coughlin Hollowell, Barbara Hort, Cindy Lenners, Brenda Miller, Nikole Potulsky, Judith Pulman, Cindy Stewart-Rinier, Peggy Shumaker, Kelly Smith, and Sandra Swinburne.

Special thanks goes to Nikole Potulsky: who read drafts of the essays and listened to me read them to her, who found the manuscript's structure and, when everything broke apart, was willing to work on rebuilding it. You *are* a good reader, and this season of grief would have been so much more difficult without you walking next to me.

Thanks, as always, to Zan Gibbs: for pragmatic advice, dinners at Enat, and for reading the manuscript with an eye towards inclusion—and for being so thoughtful and gentle with your suggestions. You're kind of a big deal.

To Julie Harrelson and Kasuna Duffey: for Saturday morning calls, de-escalation calls, bike rides with live video, and sushi savant. Thank you for such fine friendship up close and long distance.

To Kate Gray, Karen Karbo, Domingo Martinez, Lia Purpura, and Sallie Tisdale: for your friendship and belief in this project, thank you so much.

To Dinah Lenney: for always being there even when I inadvertently email your AOL account. (Why is it that you still have that anyways?) And for always telling me the truth.

To Stan Rubin: for figuring it out together bit by bit and keeping Judith's legacy alive.

To Joeth Zucco: for understanding the ins and outs of a comma splice, cardinals and ordinals, em dashes and semicolons, thank you for making this book infinitely more readable. And for having to proof yourself in the acknowledgments and fix the word "semicolon."

To the many people who allowed me to quote their work, including Judith Kitchen, Courtney E. Martin, Carrie Newcomer, Gregory Orr, Deb Talan, and Krista Tippett, among others: thank you for the gracious gift of your thoughts and work. May your kindness be returned to you ten-fold.

To all my blog readers and the hundreds of unnamed (but not unvalued) friends who promoted me on Facebook and in real life: I wouldn't be here without you reading, sharing, and supporting.

To Walter Schreifels: a special thank you for rescuing me on a pitch-dark dirt road in Mexico right after I'd finished writing these acknowledgments. Without you, it's hard to say if this book would have reached the wider world.

Finally, to Mom, Dad, Stef, and the Pea: you're famous on the Internet. Really. I'm just sorry you didn't live to see it.

Kate Carroll de Gutes' book, *Objects In Mirror Are Closer Than They Appear*, won the 2016 Oregon Book Award for Creative Nonfiction and a 2016 Lambda Literary Award in Memoir. Kate is a wry observer and writer who started her career as a journalist and then got excited by new journalism which became creative nonfiction and is now called essay (personal, lyric, and otherwise). You can learn more about Kate at www.katecarrolldegutes.com.

Publications by Two Sylvias Press:

The Daily Poet: Day-By-Day Prompts For Your Writing Practice
by Kelli Russell Agodon and Martha Silano (Print and eBook)

The Daily Poet Companion Journal (Print)

Fire On Her Tongue:
An Anthology of Contemporary Women's Poetry
edited by Kelli Russell Agodon and Annette Spaulding-Convy
(Print and eBook)

The Poet Tarot and Guidebook: A Deck Of Creative Exploration
(Print and App)

The Authenticity Experiment
by Kate Carroll de Gutes (Print and eBook)

Mytheria, Finalist for the Wilder Series Poetry Book Prize
by Molly Tenenbaum (Print and eBook)

Arab in Newsland,
Winner of the 2016 Two Sylvias Press Chapbook Prize
by Lena Khalaf Tuffaha (Print and eBook)

The Blue Black Wet of Wood,
Winner of the Wilder Series Poetry Book Prize
by Carmen R. Gillespie (Print and eBook)

Fire Girl: Essays on India, America, and the In-Between
by Sayantani Dasgupta (Print and eBook)

Naming The No-Name Woman,
Winner of the 2015 Two Sylvias Press Chapbook Prize
by Jasmine An (Print and eBook)

Blood Song
by Michael Schmeltzer (Print and eBook)

Phantom Son
by Sharon Estill Taylor (Print and eBook)

Community Chest
by Natalie Serber (Print)

What The Truth Tastes Like
by Martha Silano (Print and eBook)

landscape / heartbreak
by Michelle Peñaloza (Print and eBook)

Earth, Winner of the 2014 Two Sylvias Press Chapbook Prize
by Cecilia Woloch (Print and eBook)

The Cardiologist's Daughter
by Natasha Kochicheril Moni (Print and eBook)

She Returns to the Floating World
by Jeannine Hall Gailey (Print and eBook)

The Two Sylvias Press Journalette Series
(Blank Journals)

Hourglass Museum
by Kelli Russell Agodon (eBook only)

Cloud Pharmacy
by Susan Rich (eBook only)

Dear Alzheimer's: A Caregiver's Diary & Poems
by Esther Altshul Helfgott (eBook only)

Listening to Mozart: Poems of Alzheimer's
by Esther Altshul Helfgott (eBook only)

**Crab Creek Review 30th Anniversary Issue
featuring Northwest Poets**
edited by Kelli Russell Agodon and Annette Spaulding-Convy
(Print and eBook)

Please visit Two Sylvias Press (www.twosylviaspress.com) for information on purchasing our print books, eBooks, writing tools, and for submission guidelines for our annual chapbook prize. Two Sylvias Press also offers editing services and manuscript consultations.

For creative inspiration and writing news, sign up for the Two Sylvias Press Newsletter: www.tinyletter.com/twosylviaspress

Created with the belief that great writing is good for the world.
Visit us online: www.twosylviaspress.com

51530368R00124

Made in the USA
San Bernardino, CA
26 July 2017